How the
Italians
Created
CANADA

———— • ————

From Giovanni Caboto
to the
Cultural Renaissance

JOSIE DI SCIASCIO-ANDREWS

DRAGON
HILL

© 2007 by Dragon Hill Publishing Ltd.
First printed in 2007 10 9 8 7 6 5 4 3 2 1
Printed in Canada

The Publisher: Dragon Hill Publishing Ltd.

Library and Archives Canada Cataloguing in Publication

Di Sciascio-Andrews, Josie, 1955–
    How the Italians created Canada : From Giovanni Caboto to the Cultural Renaissance / written by Josie Di Sciascio-Andrews.

Includes bibliographical references.
ISBN-13: 978-1-896124-14-8
ISBN-10: 1-896124-14-3

    1. Italian Canadians—History. 2. Italians—Canada—History.
3. Canada—Civilization—Italian influences. I. Title.

FC106.I8A59 2008   971'.00451   C2007-906010-2

Project Director: Gary Whyte
Cover Image: Photos.com
Production: Ash Williams, Jodene Draven, Vicky Trickett
Photo Credits: Every effort has been made to accurately credit the sources of photographs. Any errors or omissions should be reported directly to the publisher for correction in future editions. All photographs courtesy of Armand Scaini, Famee Furlane Italian Club Association, Toronto, from the book *Landed.*

Text Credit: Poem on p. 127 reprinted with the permission of Gianna Patriarca.

PC: P5

CONTENTS

DEDICATION

In memory of my father,
For my mother
&
For Ryan and Matthew: my sons and my future.

This book gives our cultural mosaic, a portal into an unbiased Canadian history. A well-researched and informative body of work, that sets records straight! My children will be reading a more poignant look into the contributions made by Italians on Canada.

–Dominic Mancuso, Canadian musician

ACKNOWLEDGEMENTS

To all the Italian Canadians who, through their often unnamed feats, have contributed so much to the creation and progress of Canada.

To the staff at St. Michael's College and Kelly Library, for providing the resources that made this book possible.

To my publisher, for giving me the opportunity to write a book on a topic so close to my heart.

To my editor, for her help in preparing this book.

To Mr. Armand Scaini, past president of the Famee Furlane Club of Toronto, for kindly sharing photographs from his association's book, *Landed*.

Any errors or omissions in the information provided in this book are mine and mine alone. Please accept my apologies in advance should that be the case.

PROLOGUE

When I came to Canada in 1968 at the age of 13, I didn't know about the influence my ancestors had on this country. Not many people did. History books related the stories of places, battles and people with English or French names. Italians, or any other immigrants for that matter, didn't feature in the tales of the mighty *Coureurs des Bois* (The First Fur Trappers) or in the colonial rosters of adventurers, settlers and the who's who of Canada's early history.

When my family left Italy and decided to move to Oakville, Ontario, I was torn away in the middle of grade seven. My school in Italy was a brand new, three-storey building that had granite-floor hallways, large windows that slid open easily for air, and Formica desks and chairs with stainless steel legs. Art was my favourite subject, and I can still see the school's spacious art studio, the indentations in the desks for paint containers and brushes, the big easels, and the art posters of Monet and Modigliani on the walls. I fondly remember my Italian teacher, Anna-Maria De Petra; the thick, red anthology of Italian literature I still own; and the long discussions students had with her about the meaning of poems and short stories. I recall the pleasure I had in learning about European history, geography and science—the way every country and culture was given importance and weight within the evolution of the world. Life in my small town was beginning to take its rightful, small proportions as I adjusted my focus within the ever-increasing universe that was opened up to me through my books and school subjects.

My school was situated on Via Frentana, a road named after an area of Abruzzo inhabited by the Frentani people (the early tribe of people who for millennia lived in this region, and to which I am undoubtedly heir). The school was located in the picturesque town of Casoli, built in the fourth century and at one time was the home of the famous Colonna family (powerful feudal lords of Roman origin) during the Renaissance. Easily recognizable are the medieval turrets of their still-standing castle and adjacent church, perched, as in many other Italian towns, on a scenic hill of olive trees and cypresses spreading out below on the fertile valley of farms dotted along the Aventino River. Ribboned with steep, winding roads, Casoli is a 20-minute drive east from the Adriatic coast. Another short drive to the northwest coils up to the virgin mountain water source in the town of Fara San Martino, the site of the De Cecco pasta factory, and farther up are the snowy peaks of the ski resort of Roccaraso, on Mount Maiella.

Casoli is located between Lanciano (the site of a popular Canadian high school founded by Alberto Di Giovanni of Toronto's Columbus Centre) and Ortona, the beach where thousands of young Canadian men were shot down during Nazi air raids while trying to enter the hills of Italy's allied region in World War II. In Canada, "Ortona Barracks" was the name written in large letters on the Canadian Veteran Army Office commemorating the soldiers who lost their lives during that war.

The army office faced the school where I attended grade eight, my first year in Oakville. In my endless quest to find meaning in my new environment, seeing the name "Ortona Barracks" was of great significance to me. Perhaps it was fate or just historical coincidence, but my journey from Italy to Canada was beginning to take shape from a seemingly random pattern of connect the dots. The seeds of my early ponderings would eventually lead me to research information about the common lifeline shared by two very distant and separate worlds.

In 1968, the year I left Italy, the Beatles were all the rage, along with page-boy haircuts, lime green fishnet stockings, mini-skirts, bell bottoms and desert boots. I kept the hot pink angora sweater my mother bought me for the trip to Canada, as well as the lime green barrette with a "flower power" white daisy on one end, which I just had to have.

I left behind my childhood dreams when I left Italy, a world of spectacular memories, of views and sights for which I will forever be grateful. I lived in a kid's world of family, school, church and catechism classes, choir practice, games of hide and seek, comic books, records, soccer games, patron feasts, processions and fairs days at the beach, afternoons at the movies, vacations at my grandparents' house, and singing along to the tunes of Gianni Morandi and Sonny and Cher. At the last patron feast I ever attended in my town in the fall of 1967, the featured singer on the starlit *piazza* (the town square) was Dionne Warwick. The number one song that year was the Italian version of "A Whiter Shade of Pale," sung by Fausto Leali. Not much of a stretch from what a teenager was probably listening to on Canadian radio top hit lists.

Nowhere in my immediate experience or furthest imagination was there a notion of immigration, of what an immigrant would look like or what type of life being an immigrant would entail. The long-suffering women wearing black head-coverings and the men with fedoras carrying crying children and heavy suitcases tied with ropes or string, all of whom I saw in the yellowed, black-and-white photographs of history books or documentaries, were just that for me: images of people from the 1900s. I had read the sad accounts of immigrants in the heart-wrenching stories in my favourite children's book, *Cuore* (Heart), by Edmondo De Amicis. These were the tales of long ago for me, from my grandparents' or my great-grandparents' generations. I could relate to them no more than I could be expected to relate to the tales in *Huckleberry Finn* or *Treasure Island.*

When I came to Canada, someone asked me if I had ever squished grapes with my bare feet. Of course I hadn't. I laughed, thinking that the person was kidding. It would take the rest of my life to learn that the question was no joke. The myths and stereotypes surrounding my immigration experience to Canada and that of other Italians abounded. Sadly, for some, they continue to exist. Perhaps the outrage that I felt as a 13-year-old fuels my writing—the wish to rectify people's perceptions on the three-dimensional, human truth of those Italians who made Canada their destination.

Being Italian in the '60s, especially in Oakville, Ontario, was a unique experience that left me feeling like an alien. Oakville was, and for the most part still is, a very British, affluent suburb of Toronto, which in the '60s and '70s was rated the richest town in Canada. Although it may appear to be a small detail, it would have made a monumental difference for me to have known that the man who had discovered Canada (my newly adopted home), John Cabot, was indeed one of my compatriots, an Italian, whose true name was Giovanni Caboto. Furthermore, knowing that the first settlements in New France and Upper Canada had been aided by the service of Italian mercenaries under the rule of French and English monarchs would have reassured me as to my people's presence, and somehow their viability, in the foundations of my new country. Having this knowledge would have certainly made me feel more at ease with my new home country, giving me a sense of instant affiliation and belonging, which unfortunately, took me many years to acquire.

Historical documentation of such facts, though seemingly trivial to the overall recounting of Canada's tale, is of crucial significance to the Italian people who inhabit this great land. Because they weren't mentioned in history books and mainstream literature, the Italian presence and contribution to the building of this nation has been left out of the discourse of the country's creation. Italian Canadians were, in the words of Québecois Italian playwright Marco Micone, "Les Gens du Silence" (The People of Silence).

Italians have been an integral part of Canada's history from the very beginning, yet their names don't appear in many of the early stories. The understandable inclination of dominant cultures to uphold their own heroes as the only figures of historical importance worthy of being documented meant that Italians and other ethnic peoples were often discounted and omitted from history books. The ones who were included were usually recorded in historical documents using English or French translations of their names. In the early part of the 20th century, many Italian immigrants changed their Italian names to blend in with the mainstream population. They did this, not because they wanted to, but out of fear of racism, especially after the internment of Italians during Mussolini's Nazi alliance. It took many decades for things to improve, and today, in spite of the lingering shadow of stereotype, a totally opposite phenomenon has taken place, where Italian youth of second and third generations are proud of who they are. It is my humble hope to provide new generations of Italian Canadian youth with a historical mirror in which they can look into and finally see their reflection.

Italians have a come a long way in Canada. In today's marketplace, everything Italian is "chic." Their customs, their food, their music and their aesthetic sense of style has awoken an interest in Italian culture's lore. The wealthiest Canadians flaunt their vacations in Tuscany. Movie stars and politicians own villas in Rome or Lake Como. And Italian products are deemed precious and highly coveted. From gourmet foods and wines to designer clothing, furniture and automobiles, Italian is sexy; Italian is "in."

In the early '70s, Coca Cola taught the world to sing in perfect harmony in one of their most famous Canadian-made ads. I was a teenager then, new to the country, struggling to find young people who were like me, in my adolescent search for identity. As I watched the teenagers standing on the hill of that commercial, as they sang and held candles for world peace, I couldn't find myself. The faces of the youth in the ad reflected the 1970's media ideal of blond, straight-haired teens, dotted with the odd black kid sporting an afro and a couple of Asians with long, dark hair. This was the norm back then. As far as Mediterranean-looking kids, there were none. Little did I know that the young people in that ad were standing on a hill in Italy, just outside Rome. Had I known that, as trivial as it may seem, it would have helped me immensely in my quest for identity in my new Canadian home. It wasn't that I didn't like Oakville; it was, and still is, a beautiful, idyllic place. It was just that I didn't feel as though I belonged.

Being an Italian kid in high school in the late '60s and early '70s was not the cool thing to be. The teenage years are a time of wanting to fit in, of being thought of as part of the crowd, of not being singled out. The dismay of adolescents who did not quite fit in, either because of physical or cultural characteristics, probably explains why quite a few Italian kids anglicized their names, dated Canadians and were reluctant to admit to their background. The pull of the new society they were becoming a part of, along with the pull of their parents' culture, kept young Italians mentally scurrying on the teeter-totter of tradition and assimilation.

In the '70s, all the fashion magazines flaunted the blonde, slick look of the Breck girls. The exception was *Ebony*, the one and only fashion magazine where my Italian friends and I could find the dark, curly-haired beauties we more closely resembled. Today, thanks to Benetton, the Italian fashion company that started the ethnic beauty trend in the media, the faces of every ethnicity have become beautiful. In 2005, model and actress Monica Bellucci was voted most beautiful woman in the world. Perhaps the singer Madonna demystified the Italian woman's stereotype by showing a more than Madonna-like side of woman-hood, Italian or not. Her song lyrics and music videos pushed the envelope of what was viewed as conven-tionally Italian cultural behaviour. In the '80s, that was a groundbreaking concept.

The 2006 Winter Olympics held in Torino brought Italy's avant-garde status in lifestyle, sports, design and *joie de vivre* to everyone's attention. For Italian Canadians, being in the spotlight was a great step for-ward. It boosted their sense of positive self-identity. This was compounded by the Canadian team walking away from the event with one of the highest numbers of medals, giving Canada and Italy a kind of common cultural denominator effect.

Fast forward to the year 2006 and Andrea Bargnani, a young Italian basketball player from Italy, who made Canadian sports history when the Toronto Raptors bought him to enhance their failing basketball team. That very same year, Italy won the World Soccer Cup, with fans of every cultural background waving their green, white and red flags through the streets of a thousand Canadian cities.

I didn't recognize my own city. I had never seen so many Italian flags in Oakville. Actually, I don't think I had ever seen any. The little English town I used to know when I arrived in the late '60s had surely changed. In those days, walking into Oakville's downtown exclusive shops always left me feeling like an intruder by the unwelcoming stares of store owners. On the day of Italy's soccer win, however, a very different place stared back at me. Italian fans came out of the woodwork on that beautiful summer day, a thing that took me completely by surprise. It was a scene reminiscent of St. Clair's Avenue in Toronto on the day of Italy's World Cup win in 1983. Oakville, my new town, was morphed by the presence of so many Italians I didn't even know lived there. Oakville—the most exclusive, English suburb of Toronto, a cosmopolitan tourist attraction with its quaint gourmet restaurants and high-end designer boutiques—roared in jubilation of the soccer win, a feat in itself in a town where the only sports revered were hockey, baseball and football. An endless parade of cars honked festively while people waved and wore their flags, as if the street were a Little Italy, as if Italians finally did belong here.

And indeed they do belong here. Italian culture in Canada is no longer an ethnic entity. It has become a mainstream phenomenon. You can feel its presence when you see someone sipping an espresso or latte with biscotti at Starbucks, driving a Vespa, or sporting Dolce & Gabbana jeans or Prada sunglasses. The extraordinary thing is that the experience is not exclusive only to people of Italian background—it is a Canadian experience available and common to all. Italian Canadian culture has blended in with Canadian culture and become an integral part of it.

Twenty years ago you had to drive to College Street or to St. Clair Avenue in Toronto to buy an espresso or an Italian CD. Today you can get an espresso in any coffee shop in town and pick up the latest Italian music at local record stores. Chalk it up to the presence of Italians in Canada and the growing market for such products, which through exposure, have colonized the imagination of the collective Canadian psyche.

Italians have been here for a long time. They appeared on the Canadian scene right from this country's birth and naming and were active participants in the making of its early history. The largest number came from a war-torn Italy in order to find work, urged by the Canadian government, which was struggling to fill an intense labour need in manufacturing and the creation of essential infrastructures. Italians worked hard to fulfill their duty and their dreams of owning a home where they could give their families a better future.

Italian Canadians didn't cause many waves. Heirs to a historical legacy of domination and dictatorship, they followed Canada's sovereign laws, adhering to customs and regulations while revering their own culture in the privacy of their own homes and within the context of their many clubs and cultural associations. They brought with them a hard-work ethic and family values that were essential to their survival in Italy, and because of this, many of them achieved their dreams. They have become integral members of the cultural fabric of Canadian life. Today, many of their children own successful businesses, real estate, legal and medical practices, and have climbed the high echelons within academic institutions.

Italians took the jobs they did in the past because there was a need and because they had to work to support themselves and their families. It is my sincere wish to shed light on the unknown facts about the Italian immigrants and their often unaccounted, social, artistic, political, educational and historical contribution to the successful growth of our country.

In the beginning they started out as explorers, mercenaries, missionaries, commissioned artists, migratory workers and, later, labourers, and they have left a definitive imprint on the ever-changing face of Canada, making it the wonderful place it is today. Italians, like every other ethnic group in Canada, are being redefined by their constant contact with other cultures. At this very moment, the future is being mapped out for Canada and the world, with unprecedented new social factors of global migration and its ensuing implications. As you board a train out west, drive along one of our highways, stop at a restaurant for a meal, prepare a gourmet dish, drink a glass of Canadian wine, or sit at a downtown patio, it is my wish that like a whiff of espresso, you will be reminded of all I have told you, and that you will smile and think, "Yes, the Italians were here!"

Introduction

They discovered it. They named it. They built it.
– Popular logo on a T-shirt bought in New York's
Little Italy, referring to Christopher Columbus, who
discovered America; Amerigo Vespucci, who named
it; and the thousands of Italian immigrants who built it.

Today, Canada is renowned for being one of the most multicultural, cosmopolitan and avant-garde countries in the world. It is also consistently rated as having one of the highest standards of living. In the last few decades, Canada has become one of the most coveted and attractive destinations the world over for people thinking of making it their home.

Indeed, the story wasn't always so rosy. There was a time when people, though lured by the promise of work and money, viewed Canada as a harsh country to immigrate to. The cold climate, the strict political views and the racist social tendencies of the times didn't create a true sense of welcome to immigrants of different ethnic groups. Because of all these reasons, many people who came to Canada in the early part of the 20th century did so with the aim of returning home after they made enough money. The only reason the Canadian goverment recruited immigrant workers was to fill a labour need, and it was all too happy to see them leave when the seasonal work was done.

It has taken many years, but present-day Canada is truly a different place. Although still a bilingual country, through the policies of multiculturalism it has embraced the world unto itself. According to Michael Bliss, a Canadian history professor at the University of Toronto, what makes Canada perhaps the best country in the world for people to come to is its Charter of Rights and Freedoms within the Canadian Constitution. Protecting human rights was not always the case in the past, but today, it is what gives our country the edge in social well-being. People in Canada, Bliss explains, can live under a wonderful umbrella that protects their human rights. Here, everyone is free to go on his or her journey of life, even though not everyone may want to go on the same trip. In Canada each person is free to pursue his or her own individual destiny.

The golden road of this virtual utopia was paved, literally, by the hard work of thousands of immigrants, many of them Italians. Through their diligent work, cultural traditions, entrepreneurial spirit and constant participation in dialogue, albeit not always acknowledged, alongside the English, the French and the many other ethnic groups, they forged the way for the spectacular cities we have today. Toronto, a city with one of the largest Italian populations, is also one of the most progressive cities in North America. It is replete with the most modern facilities and infrastructures, placing Canada on an equal, or sometimes superior, footing with the most advanced countries on the globe.

CHAPTER ONE

EXPLORERS, SOLDIERS, INVENTORS AND MISSIONARIES

Giovanni, they erected you a monument,
But they changed your name; here
They call you John. And you
Look at them from your stony
Pedestal with a hardly perceivable
Grin on your bronze lips.

– Poem to the statue of John Cabot in Montréal,
by Filippo Salvatore

The Italian presence in Canada can be traced back all the way to the time of the legendary voyages of Christopher Columbus. Although it is now believed that the Vikings may have sailed to the northern coasts of Eastern Canada in much earlier times, Italians were among some of the first historically documented Europeans to come to our shores.

The first Italian to visit and to officially record such a visit was Giovanni Caboto, who explored the coast of Newfoundland as early as 1497. Because he came on a British ship with the aid of the British king, his name was recorded with its anglicized version, John Cabot.

The 15th century was a period of great exploration from Europe to the New World. Many of the explorers who ventured to North America were Italian, though Italy had not yet politically become a unified nation but was a peninsula of multiple city states. These first men arrived in search of precious spices, on what they believed to be the shores of Asia. They travelled from famous port cities such as Genoa, Venice and Naples, and some came under the flags of other countries, whose kings provided them with ships and money in exchange for the lucrative goods they would bring back from these exotic lands. The Italians of the 15th century held a virtual monopoly on the world's spice trade, and the monarchs of countries such as France, Spain, Portugal and England were interested in having Italian explorers on their expeditions who would help them find and get a piece of the pie. Theirs are the well-renowned names of Cristoforo Colombo, Amerigo Vespucci, Giovanni da Verrazzano and, of course, Giovanni Caboto.

Information about Canada's first explorer is sketchy at best. Caboto was born in 1455 in the city of Gaeta, near Naples, Italy, to a family of sailors and merchants. When he was a young boy, he spent some time in Genoa and is sometimes associated with that city. By 1461, records show that he was living in Venice, where he took up residence. It was there that he married a Venetian woman named Mattea, with whom he had three sons.

As was typical for the times, Caboto followed his family's trade. Like his father, he became a merchant, trading spices, silks, precious stones and metals with the ports of the eastern Mediterranean, travelling both on land and through the Red Sea. He greatly admired Marco Polo, who had also travelled from Italy to Asia and brought back exotic spices and silks from mysterious lands. Caboto most probably read *A Description of the World,* written by Marco Polo, and used that book as a travel guide for his own journeys.

Exactly why Caboto left Venice it is not known. In 1490 he moved with his family to the city of Valencia, in Spain, and it was there that he met Columbus, whom he respected. It is presumed that Caboto moved to Spain to take part in the expanding exploration of the lands beyond the Atlantic Ocean. Columbus had spoken of having reached Asia by sailing around the globe to the west. Caboto thought he could do that as well, but he intended to take a more northern route, thus reducing the length of the voyage. Enthralled by Columbus and wishing to emulate his feats, Caboto asked the kings of Spain and Portugal for money to finance his journey across the Atlantic Ocean as Columbus had done, but they refused.

Committed as he was to the dream of exploring the northern Atlantic route to Asia, Caboto decided to move to England, where King Henry VII agreed to pay for his voyage in exchange for valuable goods that he was to bring back from the New World. Caboto made two trips across the Atlantic, the first one unsuccessful. A letter written to Christopher Columbus by John Day, an English merchant, states that "Cabot went with one ship, he had a disagreement with a crew member, he was short of food and ran into bad weather, so he decided to turn back."

On his second attempt, however, in May 1497, Giovanni Caboto sailed from Bristol in a small ship called *The Matthew,* with a more successful outcome. After 35 days at sea he reached land, which, of course, he believed to be Asia, but was actually the coast of Newfoundland.

It is speculated that the Vikings and perhaps even other Europeans sailed to the shores of Canada in earlier centuries, but there is no actual documentation of this. All that is known is that in the times of historically recorded European discoveries, Italians have been involved in the exploration and history of Canada since the 1490s. It was because of them that geographical and historical maps of the world were redrawn to resemble the maps we have today, taking into consideration the distances and the mathematical calculations of a new, emerging globe that until their time was an incomplete rendition of only half of the earth's continents and seas.

Giovanni da Verrazzano was another Italian who, in the era of North America's early discovery, explored Canada's coast as far north as Cape Breton Island, in the 1500s. He was born in 1480 in Tuscany, in a town called Val Di Greve, near Florence. Verrazzano received his education in Italy, but he later moved to Dieppe, France, where he joined the French maritime service. After travelling several times to the East and proving himself as a great sailor, in 1523 King Francis I of France, who loved and admired Verrazzano like a son, gave him two ships in order to explore the westward passage to Asia.

In January 1524, Giovanni da Verrazzano set sail on a vessel named *La Dauphine*, a name usually reserved only for royal family members, and he arrived in what is now called Cape Fear, North Carolina, in early March of the same year. From Cape Fear he ventured north along the eastern shores of North America as far as Nova Scotia. Some of the places he explored were New York Bay, Block Island and Narragansett Bay. Of course, Verrazzano still believed that he was exploring parts of Asia, as nobody had yet realized that this was a totally different continent.

It wasn't until the voyages of Amerigo Vespucci, another Italian explorer, that the coasts of North and South America were discovered to be part of an entirely new world. Vespucci made three voyages, the first one in 1499 and the last one in 1503. He explored the Americas, naming and recording places and distances, thus mapping out for the first time what had been uncharted territory. He predicted the earth's circumference to within 80 kilometres accuracy, an amazing feat for those early times, and a task facilitated by his own ingenuity at improving the existing navigational techniques.

Interestingly, it wasn't the Italians who named the Americas after Amerigo Vespucci, but an obscure German clergyman and amateur photographer named Martin Waldseemüller. Waldseemüller highly respected the feats of Vespucci and gave the name "America" to the new land, in Amerigo's honour. Waldseemüller was a member of a small literary club that published *An Introduction to Cosmology*, in 1507. In it he wrote of the new land mass that Amerigo Vespucci had explored. "I see no reason why anyone should justly object to calling this part...America, after Amerigo (Vespucci), its discoverer, a man of great ability."

The rest, of course, is history. The names "North America" and "South America" were aptly given to the two new continents in honour and memory of the man who truly discovered them for the separate geographical entities they were.

Giovanni da Verrazzano, however, was the first European explorer to enter New York Bay in 1524. It would take another 85 years for Henry Hudson, sailing on behalf of the Dutch East India Company, to sail into the same area in 1609. The exploration of New York Bay and the North American eastern coast was Verrazzano's first expedition. He attempted a second exploration to South America, and although much is unknown about what happened, he was killed by Native Americans in Brazil. Some believe that he was eaten by cannibals, a horrible and ignoble death for such a courageous and gifted explorer.

One of Verrazzano's crewmembers on that fateful voyage was Jacques Cartier. After his captain's death, Cartier continued the legacy of explorations that his captain had started, in the name of the French crown. In Verrazzano's memory, the Italian Historical Society of America, spearheaded by founder John De La Corte, named the New York Harbor joining Staten Island and Brooklyn the "Verrazzano-Narrows Bridge." The Italian Historical Society was also responsible for placing the Verrazzano Monument at Battery Park in New York.

The early discoveries and explorations of the New World were made possible to Italian explorers of the 15th century by the indispensable, scientific discoveries of Galileo. He provided the necessary, newly invented navigational tools, such as the telescope and an improved magnetic compass, unavailable to previous generations. In doing so, he facilitated the sea voyages of new explorers.

As a result of these developments, the path was forged for future voyages across the Atlantic, which eventually led to the French and the English colonization of North America. With Caboto's discovery, a new country's birth began to incubate in the hopes and dreams of millions of Europeans, who through the next few centuries would come to its shores to claim it as their new home.

———

Italians, however, were not only explorers. Their presence in Canada's early history is also found in their role as mercenaries in the battles of the English and French settlements of both Upper and Lower Canada. Italian men were often hired as soldiers by the monarchs of French, English and Spanish armies. In the 1600s, Italy's peninsula was a conglomeration of city states governed by France and Spain. Not having their own unified nation as yet, Italians answered to the rule of the French and the Spaniards, working with them in their many ventures overseas in the newly discovered lands.

The Italian presence in the settlements of Canada's New France can be traced as far back as the 1600s. Henri Tonti became a legendary historical figure in the early history of North America and, more specifically, Canada. He was an Italian, the son of Lorenzo Tonti, who lived between 1602 and 1684 and who was a Neapolitan banker and governor of the city of Gaeta, Italy. In 1650, Lorenzo's wife, Isabella di Lietto, gave birth to their first son, Henri Tonti. Shortly after

Henri's birth, Lorenzo and his family had to seek political asylum in France because he was involved in a revolt in Naples against the Spanish viceroy. It was in France that his wife gave birth to their second son, Alphonse Tonti.

Lorenzo achieved a position of political influence in the courts of Paris. He was aided by Cardinal Mazarin, who was in charge of the financial health of France, in a time when the country's finances were in a precarious state. Lorenzo Tonti, having had banking experience in Italy, introduced to the French court the idea of the *tontine*, which he described as "a gold mine for the king...a treasure hidden away in the realm." Tontine was a concept already used in Italy, whereby the state invited monetary contributions from the people, who would be given their share of the resulting fund's income while they lived, and cease to have any fund rights upon death. When the whole family was eventually deceased, the capital would then revert to the state of France. Although King Louis XIV was eager to go ahead with this idea, the French Parliament was not. Therefore, the first tontine did not get underway until 1689, when France was involved in the Nine Years War and was immersed in financial problems because of the growing need to support its armed forces, which at that time were the largest in Europe.

Interestingly, the tontine is a system of annuities still used today in Europe and North America—benefits pass to the surviving subscribers until no one in the family is left. Essentially, the tontine is today's system of annuities, as well as most forms of life insurance, in which a policyholder, who maintains a policy and who outlives the others in his family, receives a benefit at the expense of those who die. The word "tontine" derives directly from Lorenzo Tonti's name. Sadly, after everything he did for France, he was imprisoned in the Bastille by King Louis XIV, and he died, poor and in obscurity, shortly after his release from prison.

It was Lorenzo's first son, Henri Tonti, who came to Canada with the French army seeking trade with the Native people. Like his father, Henri was an intelligent young man who soon became an able associate and friend of Robert Cavalier de La Salle, the French explorer who first navigated through the Great Lakes of Canada and the United States, and Tonti worked with him in the early staking out and colonization of New France. When he was a young soldier for the French army, Tonti lost his right hand in a grenade explosion. The ease with which he used the iron replacement made him an unforgettable character to the Native people he encountered, who thought he had special powers and gave him the nickname "Bras de Fer" (Arm of Steel). Tonti was well respected by the Native people, and French commanders sent him to deal with the Native tribes who were in conflict with each other, and with the French, in order to come up with diplomatic solutions. Tonti was a strong, brave advisor and aide in the early colonization of North America by the French.

At the age of 28, Henri Tonti began to serve with La Salle. He helped La Salle set up trading posts along the Mississippi River and north of the Gulf, in order to exploit the riches of the surrounding lands for the French. In 1680, Tonti accompanied La Salle to Canada as his lieutenant and was dispatched to the Niagara area, where among hostile Native Americans, he constructed *The Griffon,* the first sailboat to go through the Great Lakes west of Ontario. Tonti preceded La Salle westward to Detroit and penetrated into the country of the Illinois Natives, whom he won over to the French interest. After helping La Salle and the French to colonize the area of Fort St. Louis, Tonti remained there, developing the new French empire until 1700, at which point he joined Iberville's colony at the mouth of the Mississippi. The colonists were saddened to lose Tonti in 1704, when his life was cut short by yellow fever.

As well as Tonti, there were many other Italian mercenary soldiers in Upper and in Lower Canada, on both the French and English sides. One such person was Antonio Crisafi, an Italian of Sicilian origin, who, similarly to Lorenzo Tonti, had escaped Naples from the persecution of the Spanish rulers of his time by joining the French forces stationed in Canada. Having proved himself trustworthy, Crisafi was named "Governor of Trois Rivieres" by the King of France in 1703 and continued on as governor until his death six years later.

Henri Tonti, whose name is recorded in Canadian encyclopedias and history books in the francophone form of "Henri de Tonty," had a brother named Alphonse de Tonti. Like his older brother, Alphonse crossed the Atlantic with the French colonists and soon emerged as a capable leader. It was Alphonse Tonti who built the first settlement on the shores of Lake Erie. He essentially staked out the site where the present city of Detroit now stands.

Italian names are also found in soldier lists and in assorted, though sketchy, historical documentation—names such as General Bourlamacchi under General

Montcalm in Upper Canada—and a lot of other soldiers of Italian background did not have high ranks within the army, and therefore their names aren't recorded. But many mercenaries, probably of Italian origin, fought on the English side in the War of 1812.

From the very beginning, Italians came to Canada either for their own interests or to work under the rule of other crowns. They came as explorers and soldiers, but several others arrived as religious missionaries, in a deeply religious age when Europeans wanted to spread the knowledge of Christianity to all corners of the earth. It was only much later that Italians arrived in Canada as teachers, artists and labourers.

Filippo Salvatore, a poet, author and teacher of Italian literature at Montréal's Concordia University, states: "Italians have been in Canada a lot longer than the great immigration of fifty years ago. They have been here for at least three and a half centuries, ever since the St. Lawrence was patrimony to the French Crown, and that beautiful town of stone houses and red roofs was the capital of Nouvelle France."

At that time, in the mid-17th century, the Roman Jesuit Francesco Giuseppe Bressani arrived as a missionary among the Hurons. It is there that he wrote his *Breve Relatione d'Alcune Missioni de' Padri della Compagnia di Gesu* (A Brief Account of Some Missions of the Fathers in the Company of Jesus) in New France, which is the earliest book in Italian about Canada. Bressani was born in Rome on May 6, 1612. As a young man he entered the novitiate of the Society of Jesus on August 15, 1626. He studied and taught in Rome and in Clermont, France, before being ordained a priest in the city of Tivoli, near Rome, and then moving to Paris. He was sent to America for the spiritual care of the French in Québec, but a year after his arrival he was sent to Trois Rivieres to convert the Algonquin Natives to Catholicism. In April 1644, on the way to the Huron Mission, the Iroquois captured Bressani and tortured him cruelly for two months. In a stroke of luck, some Dutch explorers rescued him, and Bressani went back to France in November 1644. Despite the horrible hardships and torture he endured, Father Bressani chose to return to Canada the following year. Passionate about his mission, he worked hard with the Hurons, and even when the mission was destroyed by the Iroquois four years later, he continued to minister to the remaining Hurons, who after the destruction of the mission were forced to scatter as fugitives.

For a time Father Bressani was stationed in Québec, occasionally officiating at the Catholic churches there. His failing health and the meagre resources of the mission obliged him to return to Italy, where he spent many years as a preacher and a missionary. Coincidentally, his accounts of Canada described in *Breve Relatione* were published in the city of Macerata, my own mother's *provincia* (city centre), which in the 1600s was not under the dominion of the French but was a major centre of the independent Vatican State. Francesco Bressani died in Florence on September 9, 1672.

Out west, Italian missionaries from the Oblates of Mary Immaculate order arrived in the 1800s, where they established Catholic missions. The Oblates ministered, in Italian, to the needs of the Italian labourers who were building the Canadian Pacific rail across the Prairies to the Rocky Mountains. These priests continued on with their religious mission after the railway was completed and helped the migrant workers cope with the harshness and loneliness of their living conditions.

In 1883, one Italian priest from the Oblates order was sent to minister in the Residence of the St. Louis Mission, which was founded in 1878, in Kamloops, British Columbia. Father Nicholas Coccola, a native of the Italian region of Corsica, ministered to the needs of the many "Italians and other Catholic workers, spread out along...the railway line...over a distance of more than 300 miles."

An Italian apostolic delegate stationed in Ottawa in the early 1900s was Monsignor P.F. Stagni. The Catholic archbishop of Vancouver, Most Reverend Neil McNeil, informed Stagni that because of the high number of Italians in his archdiocese, he wanted to create an Italian parish for them. Archbishop McNeil wrote to Monsignor Stagni in December 1911, asking for help in finding him an Italian priest who could be entrusted with the care of over 4000 Italians who he claimed were residing in Vancouver. McNeil was approached by the 200 immigrants from Castelgrande, Potenza, who gave him the name of a young priest from their native town who would be happy to come and minister to them in Vancouver. The archbishop sought information about the priest and guidance from the apostolic delegate on the creation of an Italian parish. McNeil also alluded to the large number of Italians throughout the remainder of his diocese and expressed concern that many of those in Vancouver had lost their faith and spent their Sundays drinking beer and whiskey, and as a result, got themselves involved in fights and other troubles.

Monsignor Stagni responded quickly to the situation and created a mission of Servite fathers in the

Vancouver area. Since the Servite missions had already established successful orders in Chicago and Denver, it was not a great leap for them to continue on to the Vancouver area. They began their mission there in 1912 with the consecration of the Church of Our Lady of Sorrows, a branch of the Servite monastery of the same name in Chicago.

In the book *A Monumental History of Canada*, historian Luca Codignola and his co-author Luigi Bruti Liberati identified many Italian founding fathers behind English or French names. Domenico Bregante, from Genova, was known in French Canada as "Jean-Lourd"; Carlo Lucianini, a Florentine, was known as "Charles de Lusignan"; and Jean Baptiste-Botin was nicknamed "Piemont," because he was from the Piemonte region in Italy. Another Italian was Marquis Luciano Albergati Vezza from Bologna. He was the officer of the French colonial troops, who in May 1754 accepted the American surrender offered by George Washington, a 20-year-old American major at the time. Washington's surrender came after he started a disturbance in Pennsylvania, which was ruled by Québec City then. Vezza essentially accepted the surrender of the United States and held in his hands the key to Canada's sovereignty as an independent country.

In the second half of the 18th century, a large number of people from Lombardy and Venice arrived and settled in Montréal. Historians interested in Italian Canadiana have unearthed the names of Carlo Rusconi, Giuseppe Massimiliano Bonacina, Francesco Rasco and Tommaso Del Vecchio, all of whom established successful businesses and trades in Montréal. In 1794, from the city of Moltrasio on Lake Como, came a man named Giuseppe Donegani. His grandson,

Giovanni Antonio Donegani, eventually became an influential Canadian businessman in Montréal. Another Donegani family member, John Donegani, became the first Italian municipal councillor in Montréal, serving from 1833 to 1835, and he was also the Judge of the Peace Sessions Court from 1836 to 1840. In 1814 and 1815, an adventurer, actor and wine trader from Perugia, Angelo Inglesi, who enjoyed some popularity in the Catholic Church of North America, was recorded as living in Québec City.

A 2002 article written in *Tandem* magazine by Antonio Maglio states that the first Italian pasticceria-gelateria in Toronto was opened in 1831 by an Italian from Florence, named Franco Rossi. Historically, the first ice cream seller in Toronto is recorded as being a certain Thomas Webb in 1850. Nonetheless, Italians most certainly introduced ice cream to Canada some 20 years earlier, as gelato was easy to make and was a common staple of their diet. Such introduction, however, was not recorded, and an established, business savvy Anglo-Canadian took the credit. To some extent, aspects of Italian culture continue to be claimed by mainstream culture, such as what happened to Italian espresso and cappuccino bars with the opening of Starbucks.

Even of bigger and dramatic proportion was Alexander Graham Bell's appropriation of Antonio Meucci's written plans for the invention of the telephone, which Bell presented to the world as his, after Meucci's death. It may come as news to many that "the true inventor of the telephone was Antonio Santi Giuseppe Meucci, born in Florence, Italy, on April 13, 1908. After moving to Havana, Cuba, in 1835, he relocated to New York in 1850. As a British Columbia and Yukon Grand Lodge article about inventors states:

> Meucci discovered the principle of the telephone in 1849 and developed a working model by 1859. He was too poor to protect his invention with a patent. He sold the prototype of his invention, which he called the tele-trophone, to the vice-president of Western Union Tele-graphs, believing that he would be given credit for his formidable invention. Before he died, Meucci was very poor and ill. It must have been the ultimate blow of betrayal for him to read in the newspaper that his acquaintance, sly Scotsman Alexander Graham Bell, had taken his invention and presented it to the world as his own. After a lifetime of work on perfecting the tele-phone, he would die penniless and unknown for his invention. It would take one hundred and thirteen years for his name to resurface in regards to the telephone.
>
> On June 15, 2002, the U.S. Congress officially recog-nized that Meucci was to be credited with the invention of the telephone and not Alexander Graham Bell as everyone thus far believed.

This event occurred in the United States, but it didn't differ much from what used to take place in Canada in the 1900s.

One cannot think of Italian inventors who touched the shores of Canada without thinking of Guglielmo Marconi. The inventor of the telegraph who used radio transmitter waves rather than cables, Marconi made scientific history when he began investigating the means to signal completely across the Atlantic, in order to compete with the transatlantic telegraph cables. On December 12, 1901, Marconi made science news with his announcement of the first successful telegraph message. Using a 122-metre, kite-supported antenna for reception, the message was received at Signal Hill in St. John's, Newfoundland and Labrador. It was transmitted by a new high-powered station at Poldhu, Cornwall, in England. The distance between the two points was about 3500 kilometres. From Canadian soil, Marconi proved that radio signals could be sent for hundreds of kilometres on radio waves. It was the beginning of the radio communication age. From Italy to Canada and back again, Marconi was one of many important Italians who, however briefly, touched Canadian soil and had an impact on its scientific and social history.

These first Italians in Canada came from different city states, under the flags of many rulers, some seeking fame and fortune, while others came to spread the Christian message to the New World and to minister to the first settlers. Despite their own land's political domination by other nations, and perhaps because of it, they forged successful individual ventures in the New World, often leading and influencing foreign monarchs with their knowledge, expertise and creative ingenuity. At the dawn of Canada's creation, they were instrumental in France's explorations and colonization of New France, paving the way for the subsequent English stakehold in Upper Canada. Obscured by anonymity in favour of more illustrious names belonging to the ruling peoples, Italians were for too long discounted in Canadian annals of history, though they were often key participants and agents of Canada's major historical moments.

CHAPTER TWO

ITALIAN ARTISTS

Artists such as Luigi Cappello taught the Old World traditions and techniques to native Québec artists and bridged the gap to the New World.

–Alexandra Schtychno, Concordia University, 1991

A lthough it is not generally known, between the late 18th and early 19th centuries, many Italian painters, portraitists and specialists in sacred art also arrived in Canada. They were soon commissioned to decorate cathedrals and government buildings in Québec. Their influence can clearly be seen in the artwork of many Catholic churches in Montréal and Québec City, where the buildings look so much like the ones in the cities of Europe. As Filippo Salvatore stated, they are like "a bit of Europe transplanted in the northern lands of the Hurons."

In an essay on "Italian Art and Artists in Nine-teenth-Century Québec," art historian Laurier Lacroix explains that Italian artists and their works were not given much recognition in the annals of Canadian art history. He believes that one of the reasons for this was the ethno-cultural tendency of most art histori-ans at that time to elevate the work of artists from British, French and American backgrounds only. Another reason may have been that because the work of these artists was not viewed as part of a particular art movement, but peripheral and menial in its deco-rative nature, the contribution of Italian artists to Canadian artistic expression was minimized and undervalued. Lacroix aims to bring to life the early contribution of Italian Canadian artists, which has lain dormant.

In the late 1800s and early 1900s, Canadian artists seemed to be fascinated with Italian classical art. Many of them travelled to Italy to study art, to peruse the artistic treasures in the thousands of Italian art museums and to study the architecture of Italian cit-ies, with the eager wish to copy them. It was all the rage for well-known artists to travel to Italian cities in order to sketch or paint typical cityscapes and land-scapes, which they eventually brought back to Can-ada and which infiltrated the artistic soul of Canadian art lovers.

According to Lacroix, artists who had studied art in Italy would "influence the teaching of art (Edmond Dyonnet, for example), the public awareness of Italian art (copies, lectures, texts), and the overall familiarity with Italian culture and sensibility. As a result, artis-tic judgment became more refined, and Italian artists

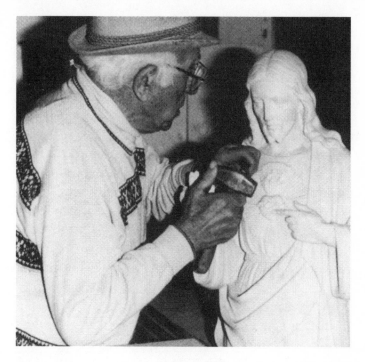

Louis Temporale, master stonemason, works on one of his sculptures.

in Canada could be either appreciated, competed against or rejected more intelligently."

From as early as 1820, Italian artists actively practiced their art in Québec. There were too few of them, however, to make their presence a marked artistic movement. All that is known about them is that they were commissioned to come to Canada to work on particular pieces or projects and that they came mainly from the northwest regions of Italy. At first these artists travelled to Canada only as a destination for temporary contracts. They were used to going from city to city in search of commissions, as it was the nature of their artistic work. When they arrived in Québec, their goal was to complete their assignments and then return to Italy. Because of the monumental size of some of the projects, however, and because of the high pay meted out for such work, many of the artists stayed in Montréal and Québec City and eventually made these two centres their home.

Before 1914 there were about 30 artists of Italian origin in Québec. Some of them were working on murals and decoration. Others were involved in the creation of statues, funerary sculpture and decorative arts.

Angelo Pienovi was one of these artists. Born in Genoa in 1773, he was commissioned to come to Montréal to decorate the new church of Notre Dame in 1828. Although the artwork is no longer visible today, having been ravaged by the passage of time, it is assumed to have resembled the geometrical motifs of European Gothic cathedrals. Pienovi himself wrote an advertisement about himself and his work in *La Minerve,* a Montréal newspaper: "Angelo Pienovi, of Genoa, who painted the new parish Church and the Church of the Grey Nuns of Montréal, informs the public that he is ready to accept works in his domain, that may be offered to him, such as: Churches, architectures, salons, landscapes, decorations, in oil or temper."

In a similar vein to Pienovi, other Italian artists soon began to advertise their work, which ran the gamut from public and private décor to theatre sets, using all types of media and styles.

Perhaps one of the most influential Italian artists in the early history of Canada is Luigi Cappello, who was born in Torino in 1843. After travelling extensively throughout Italy and pursuing his studies at the Academy of Fine Arts in Torino, he arrived in Montréal to teach drawing at Le College Sainte-Marie de

Montréal, in 1874, likely summoned there by the Jesuits. He married a French Canadian woman, Marie-Louise Lebrun, and had a prolific career as an artist and art teacher. His works ranged from easel paintings and portraits to decoration, and his work can still be seen in dozens of churches throughout Québec.

One of Cappello's apprentices was the famous Canadian artist Ozias Leduc, to whom Cappello taught all of his techniques. Leduc absorbed all of this knowledge, using it in his own artistic production and rise to fame. Besides Leduc, other artists began copying Cappello's work, and soon many other non-Italian artists in Québec became competitive. Lacroix explains that because of this, after 1860, Italian artists were forced to share the booming mural-painting market with German-born and native Québec artists. Competition became tougher as the latter learned the techniques from the Italians and then taught them to others.

The most prolific religious artist, not only in Canada but in all of North America in the early 1900s, has to be Guido Nincheri. Born in Tuscany in the town of Prato in 1885, Nincheri had always been fascinated with art. His father was a wealthy textile broker who was strongly opposed to his son's aspiration to be an artist. Not interested in following his father's footsteps in the family business, Nincheri left home at the age of 18 and went to nearby Florence, where he studied art at The Academy of Fine Arts. He pursued his art studies there for 12 years, specializing in classical design and architecture. The beauty of Florence greatly influenced him, along with its richness of Renaissance masterpieces, especially those of the great artists Michelangelo and Botticelli.

Nincheri was on his way to an art commission in Argentina, with his wife Giulia, when World War I broke out. Because of fears of a naval attack, their ship stopped in Boston, where all passengers were forced to disembark. Upon advice of an Italian friend, Nincheri decided to travel on to Montréal, where he could at least understand the French language. With his excellent credentials, it wasn't long before Nincheri found work. He was hired by Québec's leading church decorator of that period, Henri Perdriau, to create stained-glass art. Even though his experience was as a painter and designer, he quickly learned the techniques of stained glass and was soon outdoing his teacher.

Guido Nincheri improved the stained-glass technique popular in Canada in his day by creating windows that were translucent rather than transparent. This innovating technique allowed for a more even diffusion of light, which in turn brought his frescoes to life.

Although he produced many stained-glass works, he also painted frescoes on church ceilings and designed church interiors, including bas-reliefs, statues and stations of the cross. According to Ian Hodkinson, professor emeritus of art conservation at Queen's University in Kingston, Ontario, Guido Nincheri painted more, and larger, murals than any other artist in Canada.

Some of Nincheri's major artistic contributions are found throughout Québec, Ontario, the Maritimes and in the U.S. Many Canadian churches flaunt Nincheri's artistic touch in their interior decoration, their stained-glass windows and their architecture. Notre Dame de la Defense Church in Montréal is home to one of his most spectacular frescoes, while St. Leon de Westmount Church offers stirring examples of his stained-glass style. By the time he died in 1973, Guido Nincheri had created stained glass and frescoes in over 100 churches in eastern Canada and the United States. He was quoted by Pope Pius XI in 1933 as being the church's greatest artist of religious iconography, and he was given official recognition by the Italian government in 1972. Art historians, however, finding his style passé and not part of a particular movement coherent with the work of his contemporaries, ignored his style until recently.

Some other Italian artists who were commissioned to produce their art in Canada were Angelo Pienovi, from Genova, and Gerome Fassio, Ettore Vacca, and Luigi Cappello from Torino. Lacroix has compiled a comprehensive list of artists of Italian background active in Québec before 1918. The artists' names are in alphabetical order, giving the dates of their commissions and their area of artistic specialty:

Almini, M., 1870s, painter
Baccerini, G., 1862–80, sculptor
Caccignaci, E., 1880, sculptor
Cantara, 1880, architect
Carli, A., 1875–1952, statuary
Carli, A., 1881–1968, statuary
Carli, C., 1894, statuary
Carli, G., 1848–1928, statuary
Carli, T. 1838–1906, statuary
Carli, U., 1889–1929, statuary
Carli, V., 1873–1929, statuary
Carnevali, 1890, painter
Carta, L., 1880, architect
Catelli, C., 1817–1906, sculptor
Cernichiaro, 1890–1910, goldsmith
Cerusi, 1901, statuary
De Feo, 1857–58, painter

Deprato, 1914, glassmaker
Donati, P., 1820, moldmaker
Donato, G., 1908, sculptor
Fassio, G., 1810–51, painter
Filippi, P., 1880, sculptor
Giovanelli, P., 1916, sculptor
Marchi, A., 1916, sculptor
Mariotti, C., 1875, sculptor
Pedreti, 1855–60, painter
Petrini, 1880, painter
Petrucci, 1887–1950, statuary
Pienovi, A., 1773–1845, painter
Rigali, M., 1880–90, statuary
Schinotti, G.F., 1830, decorator
Sciortini, F., 1918, sculptor
Sula, 1865, sculptor
Vacca, E., 1828–47, painter

Alberto Chiarandini, renowned Italian Canadian portrait and landscape artist, next to one of his paintings.

If Italian classical art influenced the imagination and affected the tastes of popular Canadian culture of the 19th century, the Italian artists who worked in Canada gave an Italian flavour to the myriad of churches and other public buildings that they were commissioned to beautify. Their presence at that particular time in Canadian history comes to life every time we look at the classical style frescoes, statues and stained-glass windows of so many of our cathedrals. The legacy of Italian artists in Canada is visible and tangible in their artwork, sculptures and architectural designs, but like the work of the explorers, soldiers, inventors and missionaries who came before them, their contributions are often silent and unacknowledged. Through their art, however, Italian artists were able to transplant Italian culture and their aesthetic sense in the new Canadian world.

CHAPTER THREE

THE FIRST WAVE OF ITALIAN IMMIGRATION IN CANADA: MIGRANT WORKERS AND SETTLERS

They asked for nothing except work and respect.
–Fred Zorzi, late Italian Canadian lawyer, Toronto

The early Italian immigration to Canada can be divided into two waves, with the first wave being roughly between 1490 and the late 1800s. A ballpark figure of the number of Italian immigrants at this time could be 1000, but this number is not totally accurate because the Canadian census only started recording statistics in 1871 and also because many immigrants changed their names. This first wave consisted mostly of explorers and very few settlers. However, the 1881 census shows that Canada had a population of people of Italian origin that numbered 1849. Out of those, 777 were born in Italy, which means that the others must have been already living in Canada for a long time.

It was through their work as navigators and missionaries from the Roman Catholic Church that Italians first came in contact with the Canadian territory and its people. Their motivation for undertaking the journey, however, was not related to immigration or the wish to lay roots in this country. Their goal in coming to Canada was mostly land explorations and religious venues. The harsh winter weather and primitive living conditions did not appeal to these first Italians, who, at least in their home country, had a mild climate and a well-established culture. Those who did stay were mostly missionaries and priests without families, whom the Catholic Church sent to minister to the settlers and to spread the gospel to the Natives.

THE FIRST ITALIANS IN BRITISH COLUMBIA

Before a true Italian immigrant population can be described as such, large clusters of Italian migrants had arrived in western Canada as early as 1850. The first Italians began to arrive with the gold seekers of the Fraser Valley gold rush of the 1850s. Many made their way to western Canada through the United States, having first settled in San Francisco, a city that in the 1800s had a large Italian population. Some of these men, lured by the stories they heard from other immigrants of quick fortunes made by finding gold, left for Victoria and the Fraser River gold mines in 1858, and then later, for the Cariboo gold rush of the mid-19th century.

In an essay entitled "Beyond the Frozen Wastes," author Gabriele Scardellato explains that the Italian presence in BC "is suggested by reports like the one published by the *Victoria Colonist* in 1861, which described the good fortune of three Italian miners who left the colony after only three weeks with $12,000 in gold." Not many detailed stories of these people exist, though there are a few names of some Italians who settled in the cities of small communities in the western hinterland. An Italian named Carlo Bossi arrived in western Canada with the gold rush from San Francisco and then "decided that there was more to be made by supporting the gold fever than by succumbing to it." He therefore decided to retire from gold mining and become a merchant in Victoria, where he had much success as a businessman and a gold speculator.

Brief accounts of other immigrants of this early period include the name of Giovanni Ordano, who "settled near Cowichan on Vancouver Island, north of Victoria. His residence there from around 1858 as a trader and a hotelier is reflected in the name of Genoa Bay, which commemorates his birthplace," the sea port city of Genova, in the Italian Riviera.

Another name that appears is Francesco Savona, "who established himself on the mainland at about the same time. He operated a ferry on the route to the Cariboo gold fields at the west end of Kamloops Lake." The name of the ferry, now known as Savona, honoured his native city of Savona in the region of Liguria, in Italy.

Scardellato's study explains that in Canada's colonial period, before the CPR was ever built, the territory that constituted what is now known as British Columbia was difficult to access. In spite of this, many Italians succeeded in entering the region and made it their home. There were large numbers of Italians recorded living in Vancouver Island in the 1880s. Although many of them also settled in the hinterland

Italians clearing the way for the CPR in British Columbia (1920).

as far away as the Cariboo gold fields, the city of Victoria had the largest number of Italians in the province. To these first Italians can be added the names of those that settled in the communities of Vancouver Island's coalfields in the 1870s and in mainland communities such as Kamloops.

With the construction of the Canadian Pacific Railway (CPR), western settlements solidified and grew larger, mostly because the railway provided the province with direct access to central and eastern Canada, allowing people to move from one side of the country to the other. Many new settlements sprang up along the railway. Other, already present villages such as

Granville, the site of a large sawmill, expanded because of the railway, and the area later became known as the city of Vancouver.

During the 1880s, Italians participated in laying down the CP railway, especially the most difficult stretch through the Rocky Mountains. They arrived at these construction sites from Montréal, as part of the Italian stream into BC, and also from the states of California and Washington. Thousands of Italians arrived as labourers every year during that period. A government document on Multicultural Canada states: "aside from the CPR, the major railways employing Italian labourers included the Grand Trunk, the Canadian Northern, the National Transcontinental and the Grand Trunk Pacific (these lines, together with the Intercolonial, but not the CPR, were amalgamated in 1917–23 to form the Canadian National Railways.)."

Some of the first Italians who arrived in BC for construction of the CPR seem to have settled in small towns, such as Field, in the 1890s. They were mainly sojourners who found jobs with Parks Canada, the CPR, the sawmills and the Monarch Mine. In a heritage article entitled *Italian Pioneers in Western Canada*, Antonella Fanella explains that the stretch of railway built by the Italians through the Canadian Rockies was one of the most treacherous along the whole transcontinental railway. The rock gradients were steep, and the area was covered in thick forests situated in the most remote wilderness. There were probably as many Italian workers as Chinese ones building the railway, but there is little specific information about the Italian presence there. These migrant workers contributed much to the development of western Canada, and it is estimated that in the early part of the 1900s, 25 percent of the population of BC was Italian.

Field, a small, isolated town in BC, was where many Italian sojourners resided during labour periods. It was a remote place, cut off from the rest of the world, especially in winter, when despite its proximity to the Trans-Canada Highway, the road was shut down by snow and ice. Winters in Field were difficult for these men, perhaps as harsh as the working conditions. Although they were used to hard physical labour on their farms or work sites back in Italy, they were not equipped to deal with the physical and emotional toil of this type of life. They didn't have appropriate winter clothing to withstand the bitter cold. The subzero temperatures, the human isolation and the difficult, heavy work all contributed to making a lot of the men homesick. Many workers chose to work throughout the summer but returned home to Italy for the winter months. It was only much later, in the 1920s, that Italian sojourners began to bring women and settle with their families in Canada's west.

East of the Okanagan Valley, in the west and east Kootenays, the area was rich with minerals, and this discovery led to several mining booms between 1887 and 1895. Thousands of immigrant workers, many of them Italian, soon flocked to the region to work as miners and speculators. They arrived from all parts of Canada, but most came from Spokane, Portland and Seattle.

One family of Italian brothers, the Veltris, arrived in the Kootenays from the United States. The diary of Giovanni Veltri (whose name was changed to John Welch) indicates that at the end of August 1885, he and Antonio Nigro left Italy for Belgium. From there they took a ship to New York. He describes the terrible conditions of the voyage, which, because of bad weather, took 31 days. When they finally arrived in New York on Ellis Island, they continued on to the state of Montana. It was there that they met Giovanni's brother, Vincenzo, who was working for the Montana Central Company, laying down the railway line from Helena to Missouri. In order to make some money, Giovanni and Antonio joined Vincenzo and worked with him in Montana until May 1887. After saving enough money to move on, all three of them decided to go west to Spokane and found construction work with D.C. Corbin's Spokane Falls and Northern Railway, travelling all the way to the Canadian border. When the railway was finished, Giovanni and Vincenzo went to BC, where they contracted railway work in the areas of Kaslo, Rossland and other small towns. They worked in BC for almost 10 years and then moved to Winnipeg, where they became so successful in the railway construction business that they started their own firm specializing in rock work: The Welch Brothers Company.

In the spring of 1893, Giovanni Veltri went back to Italy and married a woman named Rosa Anselmo. He brought Rosa back to Canada with him, where they had two sons, Joseph Antonio (a.k.a. Bill) and Raffaele Veltri.

The Veltri (Welch) brothers operated their business out of Winnipeg and Port Arthur, Thunder Bay. They helped to build the Crowsnest Pass from Kootenay Landing to Goat River and thus became experts in rock blasting. They continued their work throughout BC in the Penticton, Grand Forks and Nelson areas.

Between 1902 and 1905, they worked on the construction of the 750-kilometre stretch of railway line between Winnipeg and Fort William. In 1906 they were given a major contract by the National Transcontinental to build a length of railway from Reddit to Caribou Lake in northwestern Ontario. When the work was completed three years later, the Veltri brothers had built themselves one of the largest railway businesses in Canada, which would see their Welch firm prosper well into the post–World War II era. In his memoirs, Giovanni Veltri wrote that "the mines around Rossland were worked *'per lo piu'* [mostly]" by Italians.

Giovanni Veltri almost died two days before Christmas in 1917. Along with a crew of 30 workers, he was building an aqueduct in Winnipeg. He fell into a well and was rescued immediately, but because of the cold temperature, his clothes froze to his body. Aided by his friends and taken home, he recovered and spent Christmas with his family, enjoying the baptism of his first child, Joseph. Perhaps because of the accident or perhaps because of nostalgia for his home country, Giovanni re-evaluated his life situation and eventually returned to Grimaldi, Italy. His second son Raffaele settled in Vancouver and had three children, John, Bill and Katherine. The branch of the Veltri (Welch) construction company that started its operation in Port Arthur in 1898 is still operating today in Thunder Bay.

There are no exact numbers of how many Italians worked and lived in the communities of BC in those years, but the creation of an Italian Mutual Aid Society, called The Giordano Bruno, suggests a large enough number to warrant the founding of such an organization. "Isacco and Caterina Giorgetti arrived in

Trail, British Columbia in 1895, when the town was a little more than a huddle of shacks along the river." They, like many others after them, came to work at the Trail smelter, built by Augustus Heinze, which was later bought by CPR.

CPR brought in Italian workers to work at the smelter, and the workers found this prospect more attractive than working on the railway, because the work was more stable and the town setting gave them a better opportunity to lay down roots. As they began to settle down with their families, building homes and communities, the Italians in Trail created a Little Italy in western Canada. By the early 1900s, Trail had Italian grocery stores and a social assistance organization for Italians, named La Societa' Mutuo Soccorso Cristoforo Colombo. In 1903, Italians living near Crowsnest Pass and working for the Crowsnest Pass Coal Company were so numerous that they formed two other mutual aid societies: the Fior d'Italia, in Fernie, on the CPR line, and the Societa Emmanuele Filiberto, Duca d'Aosta, in the town of Michel.

Two Italian pioneers who came through Ellis Island to Crowsnest in the late 1890s were Giuseppe Alampi, who was 50 at the time, and his son Francesco, 18. They came from the town of Pellaro, Reggio Calabria, in southern Italy, and worked as miners in Crowsnest Pass. Because Giuseppe was not used to the harsh working conditions and winters, he chose to return home to Italy after a short time. Francesco, however, stayed behind to mine coal at the town of Lille and then in Coleman. He became known as "Frank" to everyone he worked with, and by 1905 he became a Canadian citizen.

When an earthquake struck southern Italy in 1909, Frank went back to Pellaro to help his parents, realizing when he got there that it was too late. His parents had died. Frank remained in Italy, and when World War I started, he joined the Italian armed forces, which at that point in history were allied with the British Commonwealth against the Kaiser of Germany. It wasn't until the end of the war in 1919 that he returned to Canada to work as a miner at International Coal and Coke mines. He became a founding member of the Crowsnest Pass Chapter of the Italian Society because he could speak and read Italian. He represented the Italians who belonged to the Grand Lodge, and he later became part of the association of Fior d'Italia in Fernie. Frank was a member throughout his life and so were his children, enjoying banquets, dances, parties and picnics with other Italians.

At the beginning of the 20th century then, there were many Italians living in various regions of BC. Some were in Vancouver, with other small clusters in Victoria, Nanaimo, Ladysmith, Fernie, Nelson and Trail. In 1910, Amy A. Bernardy was commissioned by the Italian Commissariato to study the welfare of women and children in the United States. She dedicated a chapter to the Italians living in British Columbia, as she had travelled through that province on the way home as a detour from an ice storm. According to Bernardy, by 1910 there was a well-established Little Italy on Vancouver's east side, in the vicinity of Westminster Street (now Main). She described this area as one of the most poor and rundown of the city. One neighbourhood is described as being made up entirely of small houses, of five to seven rooms, which were so overcrowded that 10 or 12 people had to sleep in each bedroom. About three quarters of the colony was without any family and therefore was given shelter by the remaining quarter. The boarders, who were mainly men, paid from $4 to $6 a month for a bed, heat and laundry. They usually bought their own prepared food to avoid being taken advantage of by the proprietors of the boarding house.

Barry Broadfoot, author of *Memories of Settlers Who Opened the West—The Pioneer Years 1895–1914,* writes: "The government had all those lands in the West to fill. The CPR was dying to get those millions of acres filled up with farmers. All through England they advertised. Scotland and Ireland too. They wanted Englishmen in the West. Keep Canada British. Their motto. Their slogan. All through England were agents....They'll also pay the bonus for Frenchmen, Dutch, Belgians, Scandinavians and Germans. Bring them all in. Fine, they're good for the country too."

The Canadian government of that period didn't want Polacks, Russians, Ukrainians and Hungarians, as they were not the preferred immigrants. As Broadfoot states, even though "it is all water under the bridge, you can't get around the fact that the government of the early 1900s practiced a deliberate policy of selective immigration against Central Europeans."

Nicoletta Serio gives an account of the reasons why so many Italian men arrived in the first wave of immigration to Canada in her essay "Arrangiarsi: Canada as a Target of Trade." She writes: "even the Canadian government which, as is well known was opposed to the Southern Italian immigrants because of their poverty and strange customs, felt obliged, due to the need for labourers, to re-establish in Italy its image as a well-organized and welcoming country, willing to receive and help those qualified to come."

Canada's wish to propagate a positive image of itself abroad led the country to take part in the International Exhibition held in Milan, Italy, in 1906. The Canadian pavilion wanted to portray an image of a land of plenty, almost like an earthly paradise, where possibilities of success were endless, where jobs abounded and where plots of land were given almost for free. Hidden behind this idyllic picture was the difficulty people had in yielding fruits from the barren land and the long and arduous toil that awaited them away from family and homeland.

The First Italians in Alberta and Manitoba

The history of Italians who arrived in Edmonton, Alberta, as early as 1901 is scant when compared to that of British Columbia. The accounts of these early Italian pioneers have been blown away like the short-lived blooms of the Prairies by the winds of unrecorded time. Canadian historians have tried to dig up tidbits of information through the passports, letters and personal stories of the grandchildren and great-grandchildren of these people. They are trying to reconstruct a whole picture of what life must have been like for Italians in those early times. The information available indicates that the early Italian settlers of Edmonton came to work in the Coal Branch mine and other mines in Alberta. Some of them settled in Edmonton, working as carpenters, bricklayers, bakers, barbers and in other small enterprises. Before being hired by the mining companies, many of them also worked in agriculture, planting and harvesting produce, as they only intended to work seasonally in order to make enough money to buy some land and build a house back in Italy. Lured by the beauty of the land and the prospect of economic success, however, most of them decided to stay in Canada, and many eventually brought their families and settled permanently.

One Italian pioneer to Alberta was Paul Coletti. Born in the northern Italian town of Mornago in 1879, he decided to move to Canada in 1904. His destination was Frank, Alberta, where he was hired on as a railway worker and later as a miner. He lived alone, like all the other thousands of Italian migrant workers of that time period. Six years later, in 1910, he sent for Virginia, a woman from Italy, whom he married. The couple had three children, Candida, Louise and Peter, the latter continuing his father's farming business. They owned a farm on which they grew hay and raised horses for the Canadian Army, the RCMP and the local mines. Virginia became a midwife, thus befriending all the local people and the Native people in the Burmis area of Alberta.

In a heritage article about Italians in Edmonton, Adriana Albi Davies explains that 600 Italians in that city belonged to La Societa Vittorio Emanuele III, a group that helped sponsor an agricultural community in Lac La Biche in 1915. The D'Apollonia family of Edmonton remember the flood of 1915 that wiped out much of the Rossdale Flats. Other Italians living in Edmonton at that time included a Mr. Zuchett, who did the mosaic work for the Legislature building; Enrico Butti, who did much of the electrical work for the University of Alberta; and Luigi Biamonte, who took part in various orchestral ventures. Attilio Gatto, Teodoro Cimino, Eugenio Falcone and Vittorio Facchin worked for the Italian-owned Nu-West Construction

Italians working on the railway in Manitoba (1931).

Company and then moved on to Imperial Oil, which employed a large number of Italians. Other Italians during that time owned small grocery stores and helped to build the community of Italian shopkeepers in Edmonton.

In Manitoba, the first Italians began arriving in the late 1870s and early 1880s, with the majority of them settling in Winnipeg. Most of the men who arrived were artisans and farm workers, who like all the others, came to Canada to obtain work. In 1911, the Italian community numbered almost 1000 people, many of whom were employed in all sorts of businesses. In other smaller centres of Saskatchewan, such as Moose Jaw, there were sparser clusters of Italians.

The Alberta Heritage Community Foundation website indicates that Italians were "exploring the possibilities of emigration to Canada as early as 1881." Stanislao Carbone, in *Italians in Winnipeg: An Illustrated History*, notes that an Italian priest named Pietro Pisani had travelled to North America and recommended "agricultural colonization of the Canadian West, particularly Manitoba. This was logical because much of the western immigration came through Minneapolis-St. Paul to Winnipeg and then further west."

Umberto Pagnucco arrived on the Prairies with his family in 1907. Born in Italy in 1891, Umberto worked as a hired hand on farms in Saskatchewan. Like many Italians, Umberto did this for a while out of need for an income, but farming was not his preferred type of work. He soon took a job in a cement plant in Blairmore, followed by employment at a pulp and paper mill in Powell River, and then he moved back to Blairmore in 1916 to work as a miner. It was in this town that Umberto married Maria Battel in 1921, and with whom he had three children, Elda, Angelo and Anita. Umberto died in 1958, leaving behind his family and also two brothers, Gracioso and Angelo, who also lived in Blairmore, with the latter being elected councillor of the town of Blairmore in 1936.

The census data of that period indicates that 147 Italians lived in Winnipeg in 1901. That number increased to 769 by 1911, and to 1664 by 1941. Before 1914, most of the Italians living in Winnipeg were from Sicily. As Sicilians, they had a lot of experience as fruit growers and merchants, an art that they carried with them to their new Canadian home. It is not surprising, therefore, that most of them became successful merchants in Winnipeg's wholesale and retail fruit business.

Leonardo Emma and Giuseppe Panaro were probably the first Sicilians to settle in the city of Winnipeg in 1892. They owned a fruit and confectionery store on Main Street. In the late 1890s, two Sicilian brothers, Agostino and Giuseppe Badali, arrived in Winnipeg and opened Badali Bros., a fruit market at the corner of Portage Street. In 1913, the Badalis, together with Emma and Panaro, became part owners of the Olympia Hotel, which was later named the Marlborough Hotel. From the west to the east of Canada, Badali Bros. Supermarket is well known today simply as "Badali's."

Although most immigrant workers in Manitoba were of Sicilian origin, many other Italians arrived from the regions of Calabria, Molise and Friuli. Most of them specialized in fruit vending, bricklaying and marble cutting. One of them was a certain "Giovanni Costigan, who resided in Winnipeg as early as 1879, before moving to Portage La Prairie to establish a successful fruit and tobacco business."

Stanislao Carbone's historical findings of the Italian community of Manitoba includes the story of Italia Garibaldi, the granddaughter of the great Italian unification leader Giuseppe Garibaldi. In 1923 she visited Manitoba on behalf of the Italian government to publicize the establishment of an Italian agricultural community, and she met with provincial politicians, including Premier John Bracken. Within two years of her visit, the North Italy Farmers Colony was established at Loretto, Manitoba, and expanded to Alonsa and Glenella.

Carbone lists some of the first Italians of Manitoba:

- Sculptor of the Viking statue in Gimli, Manitoba, Giorgio Barone was born in Calabria in 1916 and died in California in 1995.
- A. Tascona settled in St. Boniface, Manitoba, in 1904 and later became a famous painter.
- The Veltri family (Welch Construction Company) built the Shoal Lake Aqueduct in Manitoba.
- Frank Mariaggi came to Manitoba in 1870, eventually building the Mariaggi Hotel, one of Winnipeg's most luxurious hotels. Frank was a member of the Wolseley expedition, which set out to defeat the provisional government headed by Louis Riel.
- The first Italian newspaper in Canada was *Corriere del Canada*, published in Montréal in 1859. The first recorded Italian newspaper in Winnipeg was called *Il Messaggero Italo-Canadese* and was published in 1960.

THE FIRST ITALIANS IN MONTRÉAL

More detailed and numerous are the stories of the early Italians arriving in Québec, mainly in Montréal, which was the largest city closest to the port of entry to Canada, where most Italians found work and settled. You don't need to know much about history to intuitively feel the Italian presence in this city. Traces of it show up subtly in that certain *je ne sais quois* of the architecture of its buildings, churches and streetscapes—almost as if it was a replica of a European city, a template of southern Europe's cultural past.

Montréal was a central link in the chain of workers who arrived from Italy and then moved out to Canada's western provinces. Some, coming in contact with the city's Italian community, decided to stay, especially when they realized that there were many compatriots already living there. Others, lured by the prospect of easy money out West, continued on to Alberta or British Columbia. The men who remained in Montréal worked in industries that required the most labour, which were in commercial sales and utilities, in construction of the city's infrastructures and in the harbours, railway stations, junctions, depots and freight yards.

Italian men worked on the docks of Montréal's harbour as early as 1895. Most of them also repaired trains and railway tracks in the downtown stations of Montréal, Bonaventure and Windsor. Some of these workers were sojourners, who returned to Italy at the end of the contracted work periods, while others were permanent workers who settled in Montréal. Even though this work only filled these men's summer months, they earned a living at snow removal during winter.

The major transportation companies that hired these Italian men were the Montréal Street Railway Company (MSRC), the CPR and the Grand Trunk. As the MSRC grew, it became one of the chief employers of Italian workers. Some of the other utilities companies that also employed them were the Montréal Light, Heat and Power Company (MLHP) and the City of Montréal's works department.

Italians were hired in the construction of the city's infrastructures, in the creation of canals, sewers, tunnels, streets, bridges and all sorts of buildings. As the city expanded, there was an increasing demand for Italian labourers. Most of these projects were performed by groups of Italian workers. Vincenzo Monaco, who worked as a canal builder in Montréal, explained that the excavation work was done by gangs of 200–300 workers, some of whom required an interpreter to direct their work.

When CPR began the construction of a tunnel under Mount Royal, the need for workers was so large that although filled by thousands of immigrants, a large number of whom were Italian, they had to import workers from the United States as well. An excerpt from a report written by Italy's Consul General, Giuseppe Solimbergo, who was stationed in Montréal in 1910, lists the types of occupations that Italians took upon arrival to Canada:

> In addition to the construction of railways and canals, they find jobs as small travelling vendors of fruit, milk, or heating oil; in industrial establishments relating to cotton and iron; in the production of bricks and tiles; in sawmills or in mineral quarries closest to urban centres; in urban building projects, particularly in snow removal; in the manufacture and distribution of plaster and wood statuettes; in stone and marble works for cemeteries; in railway stations and dock work, etc. Very few have been able to establish a small dry-goods store with items imported or made in Italy, with a boarding house, with a bar to sell beer and spirits; a few have gone into market gardening with a fair degree of success…Very few have reached a fairly good social standing and they have done so by widening their own business interests slowly but surely so as to obtain a share in the public works projects of smaller cities.

Italian workers preferred working and living in the metropolitan area of Montréal as opposed to the more remote, northern sites of Québec. They had a social network of associations, parishes and hometown groups in Montréal, and there had been some situations in the remote areas, where Italian workers were beaten up by locals. "Italians living in Québec must have been shocked by the news that three of their countrymen working in the interior on the construction of a canal had been beaten up without provocation by local people and that one of them had died from his injuries. More shocking was the leniency shown by the courts that had let the accused men off with incredibly light sentences." This was not an isolated incident, but one of the most notorious cases. It illustrates the animosity that many locals felt toward Italian immigrant workers, whom they perceived as competitors in the labour market.

In Montréal, Italian workers had more networks and felt more protected. They could live, work, speak their own language, worship their religion in the local churches and socialize with other *paesani* (people from the same towns), among whom they often found wives and raised families. This need to socialize and connect with other Italians led them to create social associations and networking groups in Montréal and also led to their success at building cohesive subcommunities in Canada in the late 1800s and early 1900s.

THE FIRST ITALIANS IN TORONTO

Italians have been in Toronto from the early beginnings of the city's history, but a substantial population of Italians is not seen until the late 1800s and early 1900s. Many Italians chose Montréal and Toronto as their destination perhaps because the cities had intermediaries of chain migration, or *padrones*, who were Italian agents working on behalf of the Canadian government and companies such as CPR to recruit Italian workers. It was also probably because these two cities were the closest centres upon entry into the country, and after having withstood the long trek across the Atlantic, they were often seasick, exhausted and eager to stop and settle at the nearest destination. Migrant workers, who came from Italy and were sent to work in locations either out West or in the undeveloped areas of Ontario and Québec, had to pass through these two cities in order to be processed, so to speak, into the country.

Cultural historian Robert Harney explains that there was another reason why Italian settlements grew to the extent that they did, in cities like Toronto. "Toronto's Little Italy could be compared to a coastal enclave on a foreign shore," he wrote. "Most railway work gangs and most small Italian outposts in the mining or railroad towns of the Ontario hinterland fell back on Toronto or Montréal for protection against the hostile countryside. The Little Italy that grew up, first around the train yards and wholesale market and then in the Ward in downtown Toronto, was the metropole, along with Montréal, for small huddled Italian *colonie* throughout the interior of the province."

The area known as "the Ward" was the neighbourhood of Toronto where thousands of immigrants lived and where the Italian community had its humble beginnings. It was located in the centre of Toronto, where the new City Hall now stands, with Queen Street as its southern border. Just north of the railway station in the grid of streets and alleys surrounding York Street, the Ward was also home to Germans, Poles, Jews, Chinese, Blacks and Slavs. The neighbourhood was looked upon by the rest of Torontonians as a sore spot of the city, ripe with possibilities of contamination, disease and criminal activity. But for the immigrants arriving there, who were mostly men searching for a cheap place to live while they worked elsewhere, the Ward was where they thrived on the social connections made with other people from their hometowns. It was where they managed to carve out a living for themselves, supporting each other in times of dire need.

In the 1900s, the attitudes of Torontonians toward the Italians "wavered between derision and fear," says Nino Ricci, one of Canada's most renowned authors. "Considered less desirable than northern Europeans—though as Robert Harney points out, their cheap labour helped make affordable to Toronto's middle class a level of comfort previously available only to the wealthy—they were often the targets of calls for immigration restrictions."

In the popular newspapers of the time, Italians were portrayed as "the stereotypical fruit sellers or ditch diggers, sunnily simple and simple-minded, without cares or woes, or as shiftless and unpredictable, too given over to their animal natures to be trusted." As it used to happen for all other immigrants and for Native people, Italians were given a two-dimensional identity, which usually denied them their human wholeness. A vivid example of such stereotypical ideas is seen in a commentary written in *The Presbyterian Record* in the early 1900s about Italian immigrants living in Toronto, which states that Italians were "strong, but low in mentality; they are warm-hearted, kind and grateful, but also hot-blooded and given to fighting and violent crimes." The truth, however, was something else entirely.

Behind their cartoon-like depictions, Italians were real, flesh and blood people struggling to survive in Toronto. They worked long hours at backbreaking jobs and then returned home to their crowded rooming houses, which they shared with other Italian workers. Unlike the newspaper descriptions of them, their lives were quite uneventful, unfolding in the typical manner of everyone else's. Some prospered, some failed and some made money and returned to their families in Italy, while others toughed it out and settled in Toronto.

Municipal records give a snapshot view of what life must have been truly like for some of the less fortunate Italian immigrants of that time period.

One, a family of eight: the father, unemployed, finally enlists in August 1915, while the mother, shortly afterwards, is admitted to St. Michael Hospital with tuberculosis. The daughters are taken in by Italian nuns; the sons are sent to Sunnyside. One of them, 13, has worked as a baker and a water boy, in a glass factory, in a chocolate factory, and in the knitting mills; in July 1917 he appears in court for stealing underwear from work. Another boy, 8, misses school, stays out all night, has appeared in juvenile court once for stealing fruit and once for stealing newspapers; he objects to going to Sunnyside while his mother is in hospital, climbs to the roof and tries to get away.

Another, a family of nine, renting a five-room house and subletting two rooms, during 1916–17, their lives one long history of illness and misfortune: the father, a street cleaner, has kidney trouble, but receives no assistance from the House of Industry because he cannot do the work test; one boy, ill, is sent to hospital; a baby girl ill with gastro-intestinal trouble is sent to the Hospital for Sick Children; the eldest girl has trouble with her nose and throat; the mother meets with an accident, is sent to St. Michael's Hospital, where she remains for several months; one boy and girl are put in the Isolation Hospital with diphtheria; the youngest boy, ill, finally dies of malnutrition.

There were success stories, too, such as the one of Vincenzo Muto, who owned a tailor shop on D'Arcy Street, in the Ward. As his business grew, Muto was able to move his store to a more prestigious location at the corner of College Street and Grace. There is also Dominic Vaccaro, who after being injured in a work-related accident in Peterborough, Ontario, moved near College Street just before World War I. His accident rendered him lame and he couldn't work, but being a talented musician and resourceful, he decided to start playing the organ at various street corners in Toronto. As was typical for immigrants of his time, Vaccaro anglicized his name and became known as Dominic Walker.

"By the early 1920s, when he was well established, he had developed a successful daily routine. He attended mass every morning at St. Agnes Church, and then at 11:00 AM he set off with his barrel organ, always walking everywhere, to return eventually at midnight. Except for days when the weather was bad and he couldn't get out, he followed his routine six days out of seven. He'd stay out the whole day at the one corner and change to another the next day. Saturday was Queen and Bathurst because of all the shoppers in the area. This routine ensured a good living for himself and his family," recalls Mary Caruso, Dominic's granddaughter.

Today, the area where the Ward was once located is the central core of the city, which houses the new City Hall, most of Toronto's large teaching hospitals and much of the financial district.

Nino Ricci writes: "it is almost inconceivable that the city of Toronto could have been so transformed from dirt streets and ramshackle boarding houses of the 1880s in the Ward, to the present-day city of brick, cement and cobblestone without Italian workers." They literally paved the way for the cosmopolitan, sophisticated city that Toronto is today. From their early presence in the Ward, the Italians of the 1800s began to play a consistently visible role in the evolution of Toronto's history.

CHAPTER FOUR

THE SECOND WAVE OF ITALIAN IMMIGRATION

The World is not moved only by the mighty shoves of the heroes, but also by the tiny pushes of each honest worker.
—Helen Keller

The second wave of the Italian presence in Canada was that of the first settlers. This occurred roughly between 1882 and 1914, just before World War I, when approximately 120,000 Italians immigrated to Canada. There was a lull in Italian immigration to Canada during World War I, and it took some time before the flow of Italian immigrants resumed, with the largest wave of them arriving between 1950 and 1970.

According to sociologist Bruno Ramirez, "the early years of this century were a period of massive immigration to Canada and of sweeping changes in regional and local labour markets." It all began with the Canadian government's realization that they required additional seasonal migration workers. Before the second wave of Italian immigrant settlement, Canada, except for a few small city centres, was mostly undeveloped and was in dire need of all types of infrastructures. Immigrant labourers were recruited to fill this gap. Jobs opened up in the construction of railways, mining, lumbering and harvesting throughout the country. Even though in the early years most men came alone to work, some eventually began to bring their families when the government's regulations relaxed on the origins of its immigrant workers. It is in this way that the first permanent settlements of Italians began in Canada. By the 1911 census, the population of people with Italian origin had reached a mere 46,000. More than half of the workers who came to our shores had decided to return home to Italy.

In the late 1800s and early 1900s, Canada's railway and mining industries were booming. This generated a large demand for manual labourers to clear away forests in order to create paths on which to lay the rails. The CPR was to become the first route through Canada's regions and was an essential route to the creation of a unified Canadian nation. Before the railways were built, Canada was just a large expanse of uninhabited wilderness dotted with unconnected settlements. The CPR made it possible for people to reach cities in other provinces and to build the connections so necessary for business, social and political interaction. In view of this, the Canadian government issued calls for immigrant workers to take on the arduous task of this transcontinental mega-project. Calls for workers were posted in labour offices throughout Italy, as well as all other parts of Europe and the

United States. As a result, thousands of Italian men came to Canada to fill the labour demand.

The labourers who worked on the railway were called "navvies," which was another word for men who did the excavation and the construction of roads, canals and railways. Because of the limited money available from the Canadian government, for two months of such hard labour, these men earned $16, out of which they had to pay for food, clothing, transportation to the job sites and medical care. This left them with barely enough money to send home to their families in Italy. On top of being exhausting work, the building of the railways was also dangerous and life-threatening. In order to create paths for the rails, men were expected to use explosives to blast through the rock.

One such Italian worker, Giovanni Marconi, from Campobasso, Italy, had come to work as a miner and CPR labourer in Lille, British Columbia, but he decided to pack it in as a miner when he realized how dangerous the job really was. He had previously worked in construction and on CPR work gangs in Montréal but went into the hotel business in the town of Lille after witnessing the deaths of some of his co-workers inside collapsing mine shafts. This was not an isolated incident, as many men suffered injuries or lost their lives while using explosives in both railway and mining work.

Once completed, the CPR operated mostly in the wilderness. The West was a great expanse of uninhabited land, which the government saw as having great potential. The CPR was granted 100,000 square kilometres of land by the government to expand their enterprise. With the grant of this land, CPR began an intense campaign to bring immigrants to western Canada. CPR agents operated in various overseas locations in an effort to recruit workers. Immigrants were lured into the country with a package that included a trip on a CP ship, travel on a CP train once they got here and land sold to them for $2.50 an acre. For the Canadian government, these endeavours meant the creation of a nation, but for CPR it meant a boost in its income.

The building of the railways through Canada's distant locations created more settlement as well as more business ventures. In the first decades of the 20th century, the CPR built hotels near its major railway stations, such as the Chateau Frontenac in Québec City, the Royal York Hotel in Toronto, the Banff Springs Hotel in Alberta and several others in various Canadian cities. The laying of the Canadian railway across the provinces was one of the most crucial steps in the creation of Canada as a viable nation. The men who worked on it essentially etched out the country's arteries, around which cities, industries and Canada's unique culture would later emerge.

The Italians who came to Canada to work as navvies came to earn a living, something they could not easily do in Italy, because of the economic and political difficulties of their home country at that time. Italian workers were recruited by the CPR and then later on by the Canadian National Railway, which is now known as CN. They were brought to Canada as cheap labour through the padrone system, which assisted these labourers in finding shelter and other services upon their arrival in Canada. The pattern of seasonal migration during the early part of the 20th century gave rise to a phenomenon called *padronism*. Because these workers came alone, without any resources, they needed the support of someone who would oversee their situation and help them get adjusted.

At the peak of padronism, a few names stand out historically: Montréal agent Antonio Cordasco, who recruited labourers by the thousands from all areas of Italy; and Luigi Spizzirri, Francesco Principe and Giuliano Sicilia, all from the Chicago area. These last three padrones were all originally from Rende, a town in Sicily, and they mostly aided the men from their own region in finding work and accommodation throughout the United States and Canada. Luigi Spizzirri in particular aided the migration of thousands of labourers from Rende, to the point that this particular village community in Italy was recreated almost in its entirety in Canada. Arriving in Chicago as a young man in the 1870s, Spizzirri was a prominent figure in starting the heavy flow of immigration that began in the 1880s from Sicily and Calabria. His success was related to the network of relatives and friends he had back home in Italy, and word of his influence within the Canadian labour market spread. Spizzirri gained fame and success by helping men in desperate need of work and providing them with jobs. Spizzirri, like most padrones, was well respected because of his large area of influence within the community. In addition to fostering and facilitating immigration, "he ran an employment agency, a boarding house, a grocery store, a saloon, a bank and a steamship agency located on South Clark Street in Chicago's early Little Italy. Further, he was an officer of two mutual benefit societies, the Bersaglieri di Savoia and the Societa Cristoforo Colombo."

In Toronto, one of the first and most influential padrones was Francesco Tomaiuolo. Just like Spizzirri, he was also a private banker and a steamship agent. In a similar vein as his Chicago counterpart, Tomaiuolo built himself a little empire in his Henderson Avenue and Clinton Street neighbourhood, where he constructed a corner dwelling to serve the multiple purposes of his padrone business: a bank, where currency could be changed; a travel agency; a newspaper and stamp outlet; a record and music shop; and a small hotel, which in 1910 was called The Venezia Hotel and later became known as The Monarch. Between 1929 and 1939, Tomaiuolo became the publisher of *Il Progresso Italo-Canadese*, a newspaper in Italian for his large Italian clientele.

Despite these and other padrones' successes and popularity among the Italian Canadian immigrants, no one came close to the fame of Antonio Cordasco. Somewhat of a legend, his name lingers on in the historical accounts of the early Italians. Based in Montréal, Cordasco was key in satisfying the demand of the employers in BC, especially the CPR, and he imported workers from Italy and the U.S., channelling them to the appropriate destinations. Perhaps one of the reasons that he became so renowned and influential was the assertive style with which he conducted business. When other firms or padrones wanted to provide workers for CPR in British Columbia, Cordasco intervened by affirming that there was no need for their services because he was the sole agent for that railway and he would only request workers through his own company. At a banquet held in 1904 by Cordasco to celebrate his own achievements, he crowned himself the King of Italian Labour. Most of the foremen who attended the banquet were impressed by the presence of the chief superintendent of the CPR's Vancouver division, who was there honouring Cordasco. Moreover, that gentleman would be hiring 5000 or 6000 Italians during the coming spring.

The padrones profited immensely from the recruitment of Italian labourers into Canada, but their success also benefited the immigrants, and Canada, by facilitating their entry into the country. Essentially, they helped these men with all kinds of important situations that would have been difficult for them because of language and cultural barriers: they gave them loans, found them dwellings and were the mediators between them, their employers and other Canadian agencies.

Eventually though, this system fell apart, because as many Italians began to settle down in Montréal and other parts of Canada, they relied more on their families, friends and associations than on a padrone. Another reason padronism disintegrated was that many of the workers believed that their padrones were exploiting them. Padrones made a profit on each worker they recruited for the companies and government agencies that requested their services, which made many people suspicious of the padrones' true motives. This gave way to a Royal Commission in 1904 to investigate and halt abusive human trade and exploitation of Italian labourers in Canada, which eventually discouraged padronism.

So as Italian immigrants began to settle, the family replaced the protective role of the padrone system. During this time period, there were two types of Italian immigrants: sojourners and settlers. The sojourners were the Italian labourers who returned to Italy when the work season ended, usually at the end of the fall. In contrast, many of the Italians who did stay, settled mainly in eastern cities, although a few settled out West. Similar to the experience of the Italian immigrants in the first wave, the living conditions of these new settlers were also difficult, both physically and socially. They too, often lived clustered in boarding houses and were employed in the dirtiest and most backbreaking jobs in mining and railway construction. The majority of them were young men who were attracted by the prospect of work with the CPR, CN and Dominion Coal. Their dream, too, was to make enough money to buy a house and a piece of land back home and then return there to live. Some worked and sent money back to Italy in order to help parents and siblings who were struggling to make ends meet.

Many Italians also worked in the Niagara region, cultivating the land and picking fruit. These seasonal farm workers lived in shared housing with other men for months on end. Their days consisted of getting up early, harvesting all day and then retiring in their barracks in the evening, only to do it all again the following day. Many returned home to Italy for the winter, but the ones who decided to stay eventually brought their wives and families in order to settle in the cities or to set up their own orchards and vineyards on farmland they eventually purchased in the Niagara region. Some of them went on to create successful wine businesses that have lasted and are still thriving today.

Edward Rinstein, an award-winning wine writer, says that although Canada's wine industry has achieved global recognition for quality wines in the last two decades, Canada has been producing wine for over 200 years. Canadian viticulturists have joined the ranks of the world's top wine producers, and not only because of their ice wine specialty. In the beginning, the winemaking tradition was brought into Canada by the European pioneers. The first wineries were for the most part established by Italian and German immigrants. From cultivating grapes in Canada's cold weather conditions, to the technical art of knowing how to extract good wine from a variety of grapes, to the process of winemaking and classifying the different types of wines to the fine art of wine tasting, Italians were definitely influential in the Canadian grape production and wine industry.

Italy's effect on winemaking in North America is first seen in the early 1600s. At that time, English settlers in Virginia were thinking of producing wine in the fertile lands they cultivated. Wine was expensive, and any successful winemaker could expect to make great profits. Lured by this prospect, the settlers started to make wine by 1611, but all attempts at creating a successful wine industry failed, in spite of viticulturists who were brought from France and England to help in the endeavour. The reason for the failure was that they couldn't grow grapes that would yield good-tasting wine. Most of what they managed to produce was, at best, unpalatable. It wasn't until the arrival of Thomas Jefferson, who had spent many years vacationing in Italy and who was intensely enamoured with a lady there, as well as with Italian culture, that a successful wine enterprise actually began to succeed in North America.

An Italian friend of Thomas Jefferson, Philip Mazzei, settled in Virginia on 2000 acres of farm land that Jefferson gave him for the purpose of growing grapes suitable for Italian-style wine. Along with giving him some land, Jefferson asked Mazzei to also bring 12 Italian grape farmers, who were able to success-fully transplant hundreds of fruit trees and vine grafts they brought over from Tuscany. By the 1800s, suc-cessful grape vineyards appeared not only in Virginia but also in the Niagara and Concord areas of Canada. It was the beginning of Ontario's famous fruit land and wine country in the Golden Horseshoe.

Other parts of Ontario were flourishing, too. By 1910, Toronto was facing an economic boom. New roads, buildings, water mains, streetcar tracks and sewer systems were needed, and one of the first con-tributions by Italians was the sewer system. Most of the men who worked on these projects lived in the Ward and were originally from Sicily, Calabria and Abruzzi. Before these sewers were built, Toronto's waste had been collected in cesspools. In residential areas, backhouses were used instead of bathrooms. Italians brought the know-how for updating this archaic state of affairs, by installing more modern sewer pipes and indoor washroom systems, which were already operational in Italy.

In the early 1900s, Italian immigrants in Toronto built roads and streetcar lines that facilitated the commute from the city centre to the outskirts of sub-urban areas. They replaced the Ward's wooden board-walks and wooden rooming houses with the concrete and stone that we are so familiar with today and which constitutes the look of Toronto's downtown core. Ital-ians were most likely influential in making these changes to the structural face of Toronto, because in Italy, wood was scarce, and for centuries Italians had learned the art of building with stone and concrete.

Italian worker repairing original 1950's mosaic work.

When these workers arrived to Canada, they soon became renowned for being skilled in stonemasonry, bricklaying, concrete paving and terrazzo techniques.

Most of the Italian men who settled in Canada usually had a trade, even if it was only at the apprentice level. They were referred to as unskilled workers and given jobs as navvies, but in reality they had skills as tailors, barbers, bakers, stonemasons, cobblers, along with having other artisan training. Eventually, they began to use their skills in the entrepreneurial businesses and services they provided for Canadians and other immigrants.

Structurally, these workers gave the city of Toronto an aesthetic facelift, so to speak, bringing it from a colonial era of wooden buildings and sidewalks to the status of a modern day city. The building of Toronto's infrastructure, more than the industrial boom, was what gave birth to the city as a true metropolitan centre. Italian immigrant workers were closely involved in the urbanization of Toronto. Their work as road pavers, construction workers, streetcar gangs, peddlers and sewer workers gave the middle-class citizens of the city a chance to live outside the downtown, commercial core of the city. The Italians paved the roads that allowed people to live in the suburbs. They built houses, churches and commercial centres. They modernized water mains and sewer systems. They brought specialty foods to the corner markets. Some of them rolled cigars and cigarettes, while some made needles on Spadina. Through their hard work, Italians helped to modernize life for middle-class people by providing them with many amenities, which, before the Italians' appearance in Toronto, had been unavailable.

But construction was not the only area that these first Italian settlers chose to work in. In 1912, Italians owned half of the grocery stores in Toronto. In spite of their industriousness, or perhaps because of it, they were not well received by the Anglo communities in which they lived. Discrimination, probably because of the language barriers and marked social differences, was something many Italians had to cope with. The Canadian government reluctantly allowed Italian workers to settle but much preferred that they remain as seasonal help. Eastern European workers were preferred as settlers because it was believed they would fit in better with the British settlers of Canada, since they were also fair and blue eyed. Italians, especially southerners, who had dark hair, brown eyes and olive complexions, were seen as racially different and were often the targets of discrimination. The Minister of the Interior Clifford Sifton made it clear to his ministers that Italian settlement in Canada was to be discouraged. "No steps are to be taken to assist or encourage Italian immigration to Canada....You will of course understand that this is to be done without saying anything that will be offensive." Sifton's words express a common belief of his time and reflect a view of people founded on social Darwinism, which placed the different ethnic groups in a hierarchical pyramid, with British people at the top.

We know that Sifton worked closely with Laurier in guiding the economic and nationalistic goals left behind by Sir John A. Macdonald's policies. They signed treaties with the Aboriginal peoples, implemented land grant systems and began a campaign to attract immigrants, preferably of English or northern European background, in order to people Canada's great, empty territory.

Despite these setbacks, many Italian workers who started out as seasonal migrants did eventually settle throughout Canada and established strong communities wherever they put down roots. Little Italys sprang up in the cities where they settled. In these areas they had Italian stores, churches and other centres where they could feel safe from racism and be part of a supportive community.

In 1914, with the outbreak of World War I, emigration from all of Europe, and therefore Italy, came to an end. It was only after the end of the war that Canada opened its doors to Italian immigrants again.

The Italians who arrived in Canada after World War I in the early 1900s were mostly from southern Italy.

Unlike northern Italians, who had prospered after the Unification of Italy in 1861, southern Italians had received the short end of the political bargain and suffered financially, because most work was in the north.

The lack of work and the poor conditions they found themselves in forced many southern Italian families to search for work in other parts of Italy or in other countries in hopes of bettering their situation. Therefore, in the 1920s, thousands of southern Italians arrived in Canada, aided by friends and relatives who helped sponsor them by guaranteeing them a place to live and work.

Other countries to which Italians migrated were the United States and South America, although Canada soon became one of the main destinations, especially because many people didn't distinguish it from the United States and simply believed that they were emigrating to North America. At this time, it was no longer only unmarried men who emigrated to Canada, but women and children as well. The emigration of Italians out of southern Italy was so great that the fascist government of Mussolini passed a law aimed at preventing Italians from leaving between the years of 1924 and 1929. This coincided with the beginning of the Great Depression in Canada, which generated a drop in the demand for workers. When the Depression hit, the Canadian government had to close its doors to immigration.

For various reasons then, the flow of Italians into Canada slowed down between 1915 and 1947, with only 34,000 Italian people coming to Canada. But while immigration almost came to a stop, the Italian community continued to grow. In 1941, there were

113,000 people of Italian origin living in Canada. The reasons for this slowdown lay in Canadian political and economic events, both in Canada and in Italy. In Canada, immigration policies were unfavourable to immigrants coming from southern Europe. In Italy, World War I (1914–18), followed by Mussolini's fascist regime (1925–43) and then World War II (1939–45) discouraged Italian emigration.

Italy's alliance with Germany during World War II gave rise to the idea that the Italians were now the "enemy," and therefore were viewed with much suspicion. In Canadian cities, the animosity toward Italians was compounded by the political situation. When World War II broke out, and Italy became an enemy of Canada due to its government becoming an ally of the Axis Powers, Canadian authorities viewed immigrants of Italian origin as potential enemies.

Sociologist Bruno Ramirez explains that "the Canadian government adopted the notion of 'enemy alien' for such immigrants and swiftly proceeded to conduct mass searches and arrests, surveillance, the dismantling of many of their associations and institutional networks, the internment of hundreds of community leaders suspected of posing a threat to the national security and the seizure and confiscation of their private property and assets. Interestingly, the Canadian government specifically targeted the Italian community and not the German community, which of course originated in the European country that was leading the conflict of the Axis Powers. Italy was only an ally. It is difficult not to jump to the instant conclusion of selective persecution and racism of one particular, already-disliked ethnic group. Needless to say, many citizens jumped on the bandwagon against the Italians at this time and took advantage of the political situation to vandalize stores and homes and to verbally and physically attack Italians on the streets."

In an excerpt from his account of his own internment experience, Mario Duliani, a former journalist for the Montréal newspaper *La Presse*, wrote a memoir entitled *La Ville Sans Femmes* (The City Without Women), which describes what it was like to live in the concentration camps of Petawawa. Duliani was born in Italy in 1885. He was a journalist and a playwright who moved to France in 1907 as a foreign correspondent for Rome's newspaper *Il Messaggero*. Duliani also wrote and staged eight plays in French. In 1936, sponsored by the editor of Montréal's *La Presse*, he moved to Canada. In 1937 he founded the French-language wing of the Montréal Repertory Theatre. Because he was an Italian citizen, he was interned in Petawawa and Gagetown during World War II. After the war ended, he resumed his writing career in Montréal, translating Pirandello's plays into French and promoting the local theatre scene. An excerpt from his memoir states:

> In an act of folly, the Government of Rome declared war against France and Great Britain. The die was cast. In Montréal, the round ups began...Those who had been pointed out, had to be arrested. And none was spared.
>
> After being detained for two nights and one day in the prison ward of the Provincial Detention Centre, on Wednesday the 12th, we were transported, with armed escort, in buses, to a place a few miles outside Montréal. Here we remained for eighteen days, carefully guarded and well nourished. Finally, yesterday morning

we were broken up into two groups. The first was sent off to prison and the other, the one to which I belong, boarded a special train that sped toward a destination undisclosed to us...eventually our train stopped in the middle of a military camp. Tarpaulin covered trucks were waiting for us. They made us climb into them. Then the long file of vehicles started to move along a cut road through the forest...Then a camp in sight. A few impoverished barracks. Barbed wire. Guards. Some other prisoners, Germans, who'd been kept there since September 1939, seemed to be on the lookout for our arrival...I find myself suddenly out of breath, my hands clinging to the small frame of the window veiled by a metal grid, and I think that maybe I will never be able to overcome my despair...at last we are in the barracks, in the middle of the night, with this atrocious feeling of being prisoners, who knows for how much longer...not knowing what our loved ones might be going through... that we will not see them again for some time to come... Then the zenith, the sky becomes coloured with a faint glimmer...Day has come, clear, clean, cool, pure!...And so I try once more to believe in myself, in the future and in the reality of the things that surround me. What I endure is nothing but a parenthesis in my existence, a trial that must be accepted with serenity, firmness, and above all, with resigned patience...in these blue and white uniforms with the large red or white discs drawn on the back, worn by all prisoners in all countries of the world, that look like carnival costumes where the clown-ishness grazes the sinister...The activities of the day are already planned, assigned, distributed...These men... will go into the forest and fell trees...those others...will repair a bridge...others who are feeble or of poor health, will peel vegetables in the kitchen...a few will do work in the refectory, sweep and wash the barracks room.... The fatal law that governs the things of this world determines that to each action there corresponds a reaction and that to each adverse event there corresponds a favourable one. The moment when all things will be restored in this world so that the normal course of events may return, will be, for us too, our return to order....Till then, only patience, patience...

The internment of Italian men at Camp Petawawa caused much psychological and financial upheaval in the Italian communities in Canada at that time. It had a profound and lasting effect on the self-concept of these people, many of whom changed their names in order to avoid persecution. The negative effect was also felt by the civic activities and associational life of Italians in Canada. They had been officially labelled as disloyal enemies by the Canadian government, even though they hadn't started any conflict. Their only sin was that they were of Italian origin and had adhered to their own ethnic institutions, with patriotism to a motherland they belonged to with their souls, and not particularly to any political ideal.

The wounds caused by these events to Italian Canadians were so deep and painful that as Ramirez explains, "it would take the massive arrival of new Italian immigrants in the '50s and '60s to change things for the better and to revive some of the community's pre-war leadership to public life." Just as they had done in the earlier era of immigration, Italian immigrants bonded together in clubs, associations and other ethnic institutions, finding belonging and coherence in their neighbourhood churches, business and in professional groups of all kinds. These groups offered newcomers and older residents the assistance they needed to meet their needs, in areas such as health care, education, social services, media and information.

Over the years, the organizations that have helped shape an Italian Canadian identity are so numerous and so varied that it would be impossible to list them all. Italian organizations sprang up in every community where Italians clustered. They were born out of the immigrants' need to help one another in a new and sometimes precarious environment.

In the early history of Toronto, Italian immigrants tended to congregate with others who had lived in their same towns or regions in Italy. They informally formed small, clannish associations with people who could give them a hand if they needed it, and to whom they could return the favour in times of need. These groups grew in number as the immigrants' needs diversified, and it was this way that many association groups were born. Some of the larger clubs in Toronto in the late 1800s and early 1900s were the Italian National Club and the Umberto Primo Italian Benevolent Society, the latter being the major mutual aid society of those years.

Across Canada, other associations were also being formed. The first Italian organization in Winnipeg was the Roma Mutual Benevolent Society, which was founded in the 1900s. The society was originally created to provide financial aid to the sick and to families who couldn't afford to bury their loved ones. Often, the local church parishes served as community aid locations.

In 1920, the Holy Rosary Church of Alberta created several Italian clubs. They consisted of men's and women's committees, theatre groups and youth clubs.

In 1954, a group of Italians in Victoria, BC, put together a committee that studied the possibility of organizing Italian immigrants, from all their different regions of origin, and inviting them to congregate together under one roof to form an Italo-Canadian association. This had never been done before, essentially because Italians usually felt more comfortable with groups of people from their own towns or regions. After a year of planning, however, in March 1955, an association representing all Italians was formed, and it was named the Victoria Italian Assistance Centre. The mission of this organization was "to promote all activities which assist Italian immigrants in their adjustment to a new life in Canada and to help them to become fully integrated with the Canadian culture; to encourage the descendants of Italian immigrants to preserve their Italian heritage; to promote interrelation and kinship between Italians and Canadians; and to encourage cultural and social activities between the two nationalities."

Throughout the country, the Dante Alighieri Cultural Society had offices in virtually every large city centre in Canada. With its main headquarters in Florence and branches in most countries of the world, since its inception, the goal of this society has been to promote Italian language and culture to Italians living abroad. Similar in function to the Dante Alighieri Society was the Fogolars Club of the Famee Furlane, which was situated in most Canadian cities and which aimed to bring together Italian immigrants of Friulan origin by providing a centre where they could meet, host cultural events and obtain information about Italian Canadian issues. And so it was that the many clubs for people of various regions of Italy emerged, out of the need for human connection and solidarity necessary for survival.

Only after the war ended and the 1950s wave of immigration poured into Canada did Italian immigrants begin to be considered an acceptable ethnic group. The persistence of Italian institutions in fighting against prejudicial practices and stereotypes gave their people a recognized status within Canadian society. The development and growth of Italian media, churches, schools, clubs, restaurants, grocery stores and other businesses helped solidify the roots of the Italian community in Canada.

Chapter Five

Building Communities: Italian Settlements in Canada in the Early 1900s

*These songs are about
the men that built the road
you drove to work on, the buildings
around you, the table you're sitting
at, the sidewalks you walk. These
songs are about two, three
generations of workers…
These songs are about
the songs
that have not been sung
the songs
that you'll come to know
like a thing finally at home
a home
like a song with a tree
at the edge of an entrance
where a boat filled with strangers
leaves no one
behind and forgetting…*

–Joseph Maviglia, *A God Hangs Upside Down*

The years between 1948 and 1971 saw the most intense Italian immigration to Canada. In a 1992 *Toronto Star* article on Italians entitled "A Canadian Love Affair," Nino Ricci wrote:

[I]n 1947, the *enemy alien* designation against Italians was rescinded and immigration, which had been stalled for 20 years, resumed. Within that time period, nearly 457,000 Italians arrived on our shores, with 40 per cent of them settling in Toronto. On average, as recorded in Statistics Canada, 19,800 Italian immigrants arrived every year during that 23-year period. Unlike the first wave of Italian immigration, this influx of people was mostly permanent. Canada's population of Italian origin reached 152,000 in 1951. In 1962, it went up to 450,000, and nine years later, in 1971, it skyrocketed to 731,000. This massive immigration boom can be attributed to the revised immigration policies before 1967 and to a major increase in job opportunities, particularly in the construction and manufacturing business.

At the end of World War II, Ricci explains: "the 25,000 Italians living in Toronto were only a small fraction of the numbers that had, at one time or another passed through; but nearly all those who entered after the war remained. Whole extended families were transported here and towns such as Pisticci, for example, emptied to the point where more of their members resided in Toronto than remained in Italy."

The areas of Toronto where Italians lived continued to grow. No longer inhabitants of the Ward, which after the war had been dismantled, Italians lived in Little Italys around the College and Grace streets, and at Dufferin and Davenport on St. Clair Avenue. Forced to move away from their country because of the devastation and broken economy in Italy caused by World War II, so many Italians arrived in Toronto after this European conflict that the Little Italys took on a distinct identity.

These new Italian immigrants created virtually self-sufficient communities within the larger, existing Canadian ones. Most lived as boarders in a house with relatives or with people from their hometown and found jobs through these connections. They had their own stores where they could speak their own language and buy Italian food and other specialty products. The friendships that developed recreated a community spirit much like the one they had left behind. All in all, though they struggled to work and to take care of their families in a new, Canadian environment, they were able to bring a little bit of Italy with them to their new cities, thus minimizing to some extent the psychological trauma of being transplanted in a totally different social environment. According to Ricci, being so fresh from Italy, these new Italian immigrants did not resemble the pre-war Italians, who, forced to assimilate by the pressures of harsher immigration conditions and the World War I issues with the Canadian government, saw these new people as "too attached to their immigrant ways and too ruddily Italian."

Italian immigrants of this time period no longer worked in mining or building railways but were employed in the manufacturing of all kinds of products. They also worked in residential and industrial construction businesses. Although many arrived with skills in various trades, most of them found employment in blue-collar work, similar to the earlier wave of Italian immigrants. Generally, native Canadians rejected these types of jobs, which created a need for

Setting terrazzo on Yonge St. Subway (1954).

immigrant workers who could fill them. Many of them found jobs in factories, in the food industry and in providing services for the expanding Italian community. One-third of them, as many as 30,000 in 1960, were employed in the construction business in the Toronto area alone.

If the first wave of immigration was assisted by the padrone system, the last wave of immigrants was aided by family. Many Italians arriving in Canada from southern Italy followed relatives already living in Canada and were sponsored by them in order to find jobs and places to live. Many of the new immigrants lived with their relatives until they could save money to buy their own homes. It was because of this support that many of the new immigrants were able to purchase their own places and to establish themselves.

Just as the last wave of Italian immigration coincided with the building boom of many Canadian cities, the wave of immigrants who arrived after World War II coincided with the boom of growth in the Greater Toronto Area, one which aided the construction of much of present-day Toronto.

A sharp decline in Italian immigration between 1966 and 1971 was largely the result of the Canadian point system, which was introduced in Canada in 1967 and emphasized educational and occupational skills as selection criteria for admitting immigrants. The point system was put in place to facilitate the entry into Canada of people who were educated, had work experience in specific fields and had a certain amount of money. This change in immigration policy came as a result of Canada's need for more skilled workers and to restrict the entry of unskilled immigrants. Changes in immigration also came about because of the new Canadian policy of preferring the entry of people from British Commonwealth countries. As a result, all European immigrants, which of course included Italians, were discouraged from entering Canada.

The sharpest decline in Italian immigration to Canada occurred between 1972 and 2003. Specifically, between 1972 and 1981, approximately 37,000 Italians entered. Between 1982 and 1991, this number dropped to 9000. In the last decade, only 6000 Italians migrated to Canada. In fact, since 1972, Canada has received an average of 1700 Italian immigrants each year. In the '70s and early '80s, Italians made up the third-largest ethnic group in Canada after the English and French.

Today, even though Italian immigration is low, the Italian community remains one of the largest ethnic

A sunny day on the *Vulcania*.

groups, fourth in Canada after the English, the French and the Chinese. In the Montréal area, Italians remain the largest ethnic group after the French and English.

Many of the thousands of Italians who arrived in Canada after World War II, and well into the late '60s, landed at Pier 21 in Halifax. They arrived on the many ships whose names are immortalized in the memories and photographs of countless immigrants, ships such as the *Saturnia*, the *Vulcania* and the *Cristoforo Colombo*, just to name a few. Pier 21 is now the site of an impressive memorial to the millions of immigrants who passed through its port.

From Pier 21, immigrants boarded a train in Halifax that took them to Montréal, the central artery from where they could either proceed south to Toronto or continue to cities in the West. This was a traumatic trip for immigrants, as it took the train three days through uninhabited, sometimes snow-covered wilderness to arrive in Toronto, and it took more than a week to get to Vancouver. Perhaps as traumatic as the desolate view of the uninhabited territory they crossed was the manner in which the trip was conducted. Train officials would spray the train cabins with disinfectant and bug killer while the immigrant passengers and their children sat in their seats. I was one of those passengers at the age of 13. I remember my father saying in hopeless dismay, "Look! They are spraying us like animals!" Perhaps it was a required health regulation of the times, yet it spoke volumes of how Italian immigrants were viewed at that time.

Today, more than 1.3 million Canadians claim Italian ancestry, making this country one of the largest Italian population diasporas outside of Italy itself. The lifestyle and culture that Italian immigrants brought with them has touched countless aspects of Canadian life. One significant milestone in that progress was achieved in 1991, when Frank Iacobucci, the British Columbia–born son of Italian Canadians, was named a justice of the nation's Supreme Court, thus giving Italian Canadians a sense of involvement and great pride within the highest law processes of their new country. Many Italian names also appear in the rosters of high-profile politicians, CEOs and academics.

From explorers and missionaries, to miners and railway workers, to labourers and factory workers, to political participants, artists, inventors and authors, Italians have been active participants in the creation of Canada. They have persevered to build our cities' infrastructures, laying down paths for business and culture. Their ingenuity and creativity has led them to innovate various aspects of industry and living conditions, which have affected contemporary Canadian life in a myriad of areas. All of this has converged into the progress and success of their communities. Their efforts and legacy have helped to put Canada on the statistical map as one of the countries with the highest standards of living in the world.

CHAPTER SIX

BUILDING DREAMS AND CITIES: ITALIAN IMMIGRATION IN THE 1960s AND 1970s

I had a little house in Canada, with so many goldfish and so many lilacs.
–English translation of the lyrics from a 1950's Italian song,
"Avevo una casetta piccolina in Canada"

In the '60s, Italy was the country of "La Dolce Vita" (the sweet life). Life was becoming sweet again, with renewed hope and growth after the devastation of World War II. This was the time of spaghetti westerns, Fellini movies and the epic sound of Ennio Morricone's soundtracks. It was a grand new era of idealism that coincided with the Anglo-American popularity of the Beatles, James Bond movies and Woodstock. The United States was at war in Vietnam, and the whole world, including Italy, bought into the ideal of peace and love as preached by John Lennon's songs.

It was a time of romanticized idealism. American culture was projected on Italian screens as never before. From westerns to children's cartoons, American movies began to outnumber Italian ones. Interestingly, it is at this period in movie history that American directors were looking at Italian films as a template for their own work. But it wasn't just the movies that captured Italians' imaginations—it was everything from music to Disney comics, to famous personalities such as the Kennedys and Marilyn Monroe. Everything American was "in." Italy even had a chewing gum company that called its minty confection "Brooklyn." In their television ads was an aerial view of the Brooklyn Bridge with American teenagers flashing perfect smiles and a stick of gum, with the jingle of "La gomma del ponte," which translates as "The Bridge's Gum." But it wasn't just this ad that reflected America's influence on Italy in the 1960s. The mark left on Italian thought by American media ranged all the way from men's aftershave lotions to toothpaste to hair products to cigarettes.

America had penetrated the Italian psyche to the point that people didn't see much of a demarcation between Italian culture and American culture. Emigrating to North America, then, was not such a great leap in their minds. Besides leaving Italy in the '60s in search of work and success, many people also did so with the romanticized ideal of going to a new, exciting utopia where they hoped their life would take on the epic dimensions idealized in pop culture. They wanted to leave their rural lives in order to live a more affluent and comfortable lifestyle, one more compatible with the life projected by the media, in a place where they could afford to have their own "dolce vita."

It is not a coincidence that Italian immigration to Canada reached its peak in the '60s. After World War II, the number of Italian immigrants was so high that it was second only to that of the British. According to statistics from the Multicultural Society of Ontario, even though their numbers sharply dwindled by the '70s, by 1981, over half a million Italians had immigrated to Canada. These new settlers who came after World War II represented 70 percent of the Italian ethnic group, which totalled more than 750,000.

World War II had a devastating effect on Italy's economy, but by the '60s, things began to improve. Even though the development of the Italian economy after World War II was a success story for many Italians, it was not the case for all Italians. Economic growth accelerated between 1950 and 1963, but it was mostly in northern Italy, where businesses and factories were already in place. Before the war and to the present day, most of Italy's commercial centres were in the northern regions, which were much more developed than the rural south. Because of the resulting poverty in Italy's south, large numbers of people had to leave the country for other shores and to Canada.

The large exodus of Italians toward Canada was also related to Italy's change from being an agriculturally based economy to an industrial one. As the industry in cities increased, agriculture began to decline, a phenomenon that overtook all of Europe. Because industry was situated mostly in the cities to the north, the people who lived in the agricultural, rural centres of the south found themselves in a dire situation. Most affected of all were the people who didn't own land. In the post-war era of Italy, southerners were basically forced to leave their native land to search for employment, out of the sheer need to survive. Rural and agricultural life had lost the competition with urban industry, and because of better education, mechanization and higher productivity, the southern countryside was abandoned in favour of a higher standard of living. With increased urbanization came an increasing need for labourers in a variety of industries, especially in undesirable ones. Southern Italians began to emigrate to northern Italian cities and to other European countries such as France, Belgium and Germany and across the ocean to Canada, the United States and Australia.

Even though mainland Italy's production grew by an average of six percent per year in the period between 1950 and 1963, hundreds of thousands of people had to leave the country to better their own personal, financial situation. During this period, when thousands of southerners were emigrating, Italy's actual industrial output peaked at over 10 percent per year, a rate surpassed only by Japan and West Germany. The country enjoyed virtually full employment, and in 1963, investment reached 27 percent of that year's revenue. The success was in part due to the decision of the Italian government to promote free-market policies and to open up international trade. Italy was an enthusiastic member of the common market right from the beginning, and its membership favoured the Italian manufacturing industry, which expanded enormously. Some of the most renowned Italian products at this time were Olivetti typewriters and FIAT automobiles.

The province of Ontario, which was experiencing a boom in industry and the construction business, was the main destination of Italian immigrants. They came to Ontario mostly as manual labourers. Within the province, Toronto was the major destination for Italians. By 1981, building on a pre-war community of about 16,000 people, the new Italian influx into the city boosted the community's numbers to 300,000. This was twice the number of Italians found in the Montréal area and second only to Sault Ste. Marie, where Italians formed a concentrated, though small group. Regardless, according to the census of 1981, Metropolitan Toronto was home to about 40 percent of Canada's Italians.

In the late '50s, immigration officials, politicians and journalists expressed a growing alarm that for the first time in Canada's history, an ethnic group had surpassed British immigration. In 1962, the Conservative cabinet passed an order to restrict the sponsorship of European immigrants (who at that time were mostly Italians) to immediate family members.

As writer Robert Harney explains: "this act passed by the Canadian government was a signal on the part of the politicians of their attempt to control the numbers of Italians coming into the country." They feared the political consequences their presence could have down the road. What they recognized was that those immigrants had become a political entity and could be a threat to the mainstream status quo. It was at this point in time and for this very reason that Canada closed its doors to European immigrants and opened them to the ones from Commonwealth countries. This was a crucial step in changing the social makeup of Canada. What had been a population of mostly English, French and Italian immigrants gave way to the multiethnic mix we have today.

Italian workers at the Cooksville Brick Company in Ontario.

If in the '60s and '70s Italians were the third-largest ethnic group in Canada, their presence must have had a strong effect on the fabric of their new country. By 1971 there were 730,820 Canadians of Italian origin in Canada. Of that number, 160,600 lived in Montréal, and 271,755 in Toronto, while British Columbia was home to 30,045 Italian Canadians. Because of their large numbers in Toronto and Montréal, Italians made their greatest, immediate impact in these cities, though their presence, in even minimal numbers, was felt throughout Canada's provinces.

In the '50s, thousands of Italians had come into the country with government-issued calls for workers, for short-term contracts. They had come as farm help, railway workers, lumberjacks, miners, and in the case of women, as domestics. The Italians who came in the

'60s, however, came with the intention to stay. Their presence was particularly felt in the building of our cities' infrastructures and identities.

Italians were hired in the construction industry in large numbers as semi-skilled or unskilled labourers. Eventually, with training on the job from other Italians, these new immigrants became skilled tradesmen. Many of them formed numerous partnerships and small limited companies as contractors and subcontractors. In Toronto, 15,560 Italians worked in construction, which was one-third of the entire industry's workforce. Eighty-five percent of the city's tradesmen were Italians working in residential bricklaying. In the decades of their highest entry to the country, Italians comprised most of the labour workforce in residential, commercial and industrial construction.

These workers were often underpaid for difficult and backbreaking labour. In addition, the work sites were often unsafe, and they had no legal recourse. Employers were known to cheat them out of their overtime and vacation pay, using the threat of dismissal should they report it. Canadian workers who had been in the construction business longer resented these Italian workers and didn't like them to enter into their unions. It took a tragic accident in North Toronto's Hogg's Hollow in 1960 to change things. A front-page headline of the *Toronto Daily Star* read:

Hope Gone for Four Trapped Under Don

Rescue workers probed the silt and mud of a sealed drainage tunnel under the Don River today, in a non-stop effort to find four men entombed last night when a flash fire blocked their escape.

There was almost no hope of finding them alive.

The body of one man who had been working with the other four was brought to the surface early this morning. He was Pasquale Allegretta, 27, of Normandy Ave.

A sixth man was rescued from the 30 foot-deep tunnel.

When the welding crew was at work last night, a spark from a welding torch started the fire.

The trapped men were identified as Giovanni Puglia, 23, of Palmerston Ave., John Correglio, 30, of Yonge St., Alessandro Mantella, 25, of Palmerston Ave., and his brother Guido, 23.

There was no hope for these young men who were buried alive in the Hogg's Hollow water main shaft. But their deaths were not an isolated incident. As Nino Ricci explains: "they were merely more glaring examples in a long, quiet litany of injury and death; but they were significant both in arousing a public outcry and in galvanizing the Italian community itself." An inquest that followed the accident showed that despite many protests by the foremen of the Hogg's Hollow project, safety regulations had been blindly ignored. The accident spurred Italians to organize their labour activity. Many strikes followed, leading to a provincial inquiry of the incident. Two men, Bruno Zanini and John Stefanini, led labourers in work protests against unsafe and unfair working conditions. Stefanini was actually sent to jail because of his strike activities. The positive outcome of the tragedy, however, was the legislation of the many safety regulations for construction and industry workers in Ontario. It was the catalyst for a massive revision of

Ontario's labour laws, which were put in place in order to ensure basic safety provisions for workers and to set a standard minimum wage.

Hundreds of thousands of Italians came to Toronto because of the city's local economy. Already considered the richest Canadian city with the most political and industrial influence, Toronto became even more powerful. In the '40s, Toronto and its suburbs had most of the manufacturing force and purchasing power in the province. The tremendous energy supplies of Ontario also gave rise to large investments into the province's companies. Toronto became the coveted destination, attracting labour from within Canada and from countries overseas.

The Italians who entered Canada in the '60s and in the early '70s worked as carpenters, bricklayers, plasterers, cement workers and stonemasons. Some of them were already trained for such trades in Italy and some were not, but they were willing to work at such jobs in order to provide financial stability and a home for their families.

Their predecessors had come to Canada in the early part of the 20th century and had chopped down forests, laid down railways and dug coal and metals from mine shafts, but these more contemporary Italian immigrants virtually built the city of Toronto with their hands. Whether working for already established building companies or as independent contractors, Italian immigrant men during the '60s, '70s and well into the '80s built much of the suburban housing in the Greater Toronto Area. If their names do not appear in the rosters of who's who in the architecture of that period, it is because their contribution was mostly at the construction level. Under the management of

Canadian architects and engineers, this largely Italian labour force built the CN tower, the Skydome (now known as the Rogers Centre) and most of the skyscrapers in the downtown core of the city.

The many Italian workers who were seriously injured or lost their lives on work sites around Toronto are now recognized as heroes by the new generations of Italians who understand their parents' sacrifice. The five Italian men who lost their lives at Hogg's Hollow in 1960 are remembered with a plaque at the accident site. Known as "Breaking Ground," COSTI's Hogg's Hollow Memorial was created by Laura Swim. In 1999, Mel Lastman, the former mayor of Toronto, proclaimed April 28 as "National Day of Mourning" in memory of the workers who had been killed, injured or disabled at their place of work. In 2005, two ceremonies were held in remembrance of Italian workers who had been injured or killed on the job: one at Larry Sefton Park, behind Toronto's City Hall, and the other at the Memorial Arena in Woodbridge, where a monument to Italian workers was unveiled. These ceremonies were a big step toward acknowledging the great sacrifices that Italian workers made in the building of Canadian cities. Since Mel Lastman's declaration of the National Day of Mourning, people in 70 countries now observe April 28 as a day of mourning for their workers, a clear sign that Italian Canadians had a great effect on society and the world at large.

CHAPTER SEVEN

THE ROLE OF ITALIAN WOMEN IN CANADA

*Within the patriarchal framework of the family, Italian
women performed demanding roles as immigrants,
workers, wives and mothers. Their active commitment to
the family helped bridge the move from the Old World
to the New, as women's labour, both paid and unpaid,
continued to help ensure the survival and material well-
being of their families.*

–Franca Iacovetta

I n the early decades of Italian immigration to Canada, men played a major role in the building of the
country's infrastructures. Their toil and mass sacrifice, along with that of other immigrants, paved the
virgin forests of this cold paradise into the highways,
railways and cities we see today. The first Italian men
came alone. For the most part, they were young, single men who came to Canada to make a fortune and
then would go back to Italy, where they had left their

families, their women, their hearts. By 1931, however, the Italian women who began arriving to Canada soon outnumbered men. Like their male counterparts, they also came with the incentive of building a better life. Some were single women, often sent for as brides by the single male navvies and settlers, but most arrived with their husbands and families.

The first years of immigration were probably harder on women than they were on men. They had the multiple tasks of running the household, as well as caring for boarders, preparing meals, washing laundry, taking care of children, tending to a vegetable garden and preparing tomato sauce and other bottled preserves in the fall, which helped to minimize the cost of food for the family. And on top of all these chores, most of these women also worked outside the home, either as domestics, as workers in factories or in garment sweatshops.

Grace Bagnato arrived in Toronto's Ward area with her family in 1896. Because she bore 13 children, she received a prize of $500,000 from the estate of a Toronto attorney, Charles Vance Millar, who had promised to give this monetary prize to the first woman to have the most children in Toronto in the 10-year period after his death. Grace Bagnato happened to be the lucky woman, and she became a bit of a legend because of this, but it wasn't the only reason. Bagnato had an aptitude for learning languages and managed to learn six languages on top of being fluent in Italian and English. Living in the Ward, she came in contact with people of many and varied ethnic groups, and she used her linguistic versatility to assist them with translations, as well as helping them with all sorts of other issues.

She became an aid to her Italian compatriots as well as to other immigrants who needed a helping hand in their new, foreign environment. She dabbled in political issues, was an interpreter in court and spoke out on behalf of underprivileged people. Because of her selfless dedication to others, Bagnato was awarded a car by the Italian community. Her son Vince has stated that besides being a wonderful mother, Grace was definitely one of the first seeds of multiculturalism in Canada.

In the town of Field, BC, the first Italian women arrived around 1920. By this point in time, the men employed by CPR, Monarch Mines and other western companies had decided to settle, and they sent for their wives and children to join them out west. Coming from southern regions of Italy, where the climate is mild, these women were shocked by the extreme cold temperatures. They were also shocked by the difference in culture, or lack thereof. Imagine living all your life in a place where spring begins in February and ends in November. Imagine winters so mild that it only snows on the highest mountain peaks, and where orange and lemon groves thrive for most of the year. The women left villages of kindred townsfolk, where everyone knows your name and with whom you can share your joys and woes, knowing that if you need a hand, they're always there for you—from your parents and siblings to extended families, school friends and neighbours.

Now imagine the 10-day journey to Canada across the Atlantic. The ship constantly sways while every breath you take is infused with the salty smell of the ocean. Seasickness is inevitable as you anxiously anticipate stepping off the rocking motion of the water onto solid land to finally be reunited with your husband. Now, imagine your surprise when you realize it will take you another 10 days to get from Halifax to British Columbia, 10 more days of train travel across uninhabited wilderness. For those women arriving at their new homes, it must have felt as though they had landed on the moon. Outside of their immediate settlements, their destination might as well have been the moon, with its immense landscapes of uninhabited wilderness, mountains and stretches of forests, which became even bleaker with the coming of winter and its ice storms, subzero temperatures and deep snow that lasted for months on end.

If they had dreamed of a better future, like many other immigrant women who settled the West, they were faced with greater hardships than they had faced back home. Working and taking care of their families were tasks compounded by the lack of traditional support systems of relatives, networks of friends and associations. The biggest challenge Italian women had to face once they arrived in Canada was the deep sense of social alienation, and for women, especially southern Italian women, who culturally thrived on connection, this was a difficult issue to surmount. Without much option for a different life, they had to cope and rise to the occasion. They could not give up, for their families' sake, so they had to make the best of it.

As Antonella Fanella writes in the article *Italian Pioneers in Western Canada*, these women "confronted their situation with savvy and managed to carve a life for their families virtually out of nothing. They rose to the hardships of life in the Rockies. They were innovative and hardworking. They grew vegetables and flowers in gardens where previously only weeds had grown. Window boxes came alive with Italian herbs. They kept chickens in their backyards and introduced Field to delightful Italian dishes. They even made their own wine from grapes ordered from Italian grocery stores in Calgary. Against the odds, they managed to recreate as much of the old culture as they could."

These women's lives centred around family, friends and religion, just as they had done in their towns in Italy. "They attended St. Joseph's, a small Catholic church built in 1905. They didn't have their own parish priest in Field, so the parishioners had to wait for the five o'clock mass every Sunday because the priest had to come from another town. But they waited and in fact, the little church was packed every Sunday evening at five o'clock." It was their way of maintaining a sense of meaning and order within the uncertainty of a new land, by adhering to their faith values and by congregating with other Italians, thus sharing in the social life that was so precious to them in order to survive.

One resident of Field, writes Fanella, "recalled having dinner with a family from Italy where she was served homemade pasta with a ragu that the woman had made with tomatoes from her own backyard. What impressed her more than the delicious food was how this family managed to grow tomatoes in such a harsh climate." And that's what these women did. They grew gardens, and families, in places that to them seemed to be uninhabitable or uncultivable, They managed to create something out of nothing.

Italian women were no strangers to work. In Italy many of them had juggled farm work, house chores and raising families. Many of them had vocational experience in sewing, embroidering and the management of small family businesses. They played strong roles within their homes and their communities. Even though Italian women came from what was viewed to be a patriarchal family system, they had a strong voice within the family. Even in fascist times, women were recognized by Mussolini as an important part of the Italian society, and they formed their own political and religious groups. Despite coming from a traditional family culture, Italian women were used to congregating with each other in church associations, in cultural clubs and in the organization of town celebrations. They often gathered with other women in the preparation of food and activities for special feasts. When they came to Canada, they applied these skills of organization and community life to the many new Canadian churches and cultural club associations in which they participated. Through such organizations, Italian women played a major role in keeping their cultural flame alive.

The Famee Furlane Women's Group is an example of a very successful Italian women's organization that started in Toronto but now has corollary branches all throughout Canada. The women from the Friuli Venezia Giulia region in Italy founded "La Societa Femminile Friulana" in May 1938, in Toronto. The original founders were 28 women who wanted a meeting place just like their husbands, who had their own "Fogolars" club, in order to overcome the isolation of being home alone. Through their organization, the women planned special event celebrations for their families and their community to try to keep their traditions and customs alive, not only for themselves but also for their children. Today, their association continues to foster

Societa Femminile celebrating Canada's centennial (1967).

the perpetuation of their customs. They have also moved on to fundraising campaigns that aim to help and contribute to the larger Canadian community. Their venue has expanded to fund artistic, cultural and sports endeavours through their own centre and other associations, such as the Columbus Centre, the Italian Cultural Institute and the University of Toronto. Although the Famee Furlane's women's club in Toronto is one of the largest and best-organized Italian women's clubs in Canada, there are many other, if smaller, but nonetheless influential, Italian women's clubs throughout the country.

Roberto Perin, from the Department of History at York University, writes: "Women are a vital part of the immigrant constituency. The traditional cliché of the Southern peasant, usually supported by foreign sociologists and anthropologists, was that of a passive, submissive, and conservative being. This couldn't be further from the truth." Two essays by Franc Sturino and Franca Iacovetta on the Italian immigrant woman in Canada have dispelled this caricature:

Working within the traditional constraints of their culture, with its strict gender roles, women could influence, cajole or dominate their husbands and thus be a power to be reckoned with within the family unit. They were actively involved in the decision-making process concerning emigration and at times determined it. Neither in the Old World nor in the New was their universe strictly circumscribed by the hearth. In the Mezzogiorno, (the central/south of Italy) their casual involvement in cottage industries among other things brought them into contact with a broader world. In Canada, their proportionately large participation in the active labour force after World War II provided additional opportunities to expand their horizons.

The efforts and contributions of Italian women helped solidify the Italian community in Canada, and they warrant them full membership in the historical process of the country. Anna Makolkin, a professor of comparative literature at the University of Toronto, explains that Italian women brought their sense of beauty and style to Canada, along with their great professional and organizational skills. Even though they came from rural areas, the towns where they lived were historical, cultural centres. They were already functioning in cities and small towns that had been civilized for thousands of years. Despite the poor circumstances of the people who had to emigrate, their towns could definitely not be compared to the rural, colonial village culture of Canada. When these women immigrated to Canada, they lost the aesthetic beauty of their cities and habitat. They suddenly found themselves in a pioneer culture, even though living in urban centres. Canadian cities were not the same as Italian cities or even small towns. Buildings were makeshift and functional. There were no meeting places, and these women found themselves socially alienated. As far as fashion was concerned, it was the same. Canadians dressed for warmth and comfort, while in Italy, style was also important.

Italian women brought to attention the need for beautification, in home building and fashion. To fulfill this need, many Italian businesses began importing items used in Italy, such as marble, granite and ceramic, to give homes a more beautiful look. Similarly, others imported Italian fabrics and fashion items, which began to revolutionize our fashion industry, from the garment shops of Montréal, Canada's fashion capital, to the fashion district on Spadina in Toronto, eventually making its way to the downtowns of every city. Suddenly, the booming home construction business began putting out home designs that were much more similar to European homes than to the old Canadian dwellings of the '50s and '60s. Large bathrooms, entrances and kitchens began to resemble the open concept spaces of Italian villas and large country homes, replacing the small hallways and tiny bathrooms of past Canadian design. Suddenly, Italian kitchens and bathrooms became all the rage, along with Italian leather sofas and chairs. If much of the current house design, home décor and clothing industry has changed, it was definitely influenced by the

Socializing at an upholstery factory.

Italian touch of the people who helped design and manufacture them.

Many Italian women who arrived in Canada in the '60s worked in manufacturing businesses. They were hired in factories as seamstresses alongside Jewish women, for what was to become Canada's hub in the fashion industry. The women worked in clothing manufacturing both in Montréal and Toronto. What is now known as Chinatown along Spadina used to be the garment district of Toronto. Thousands of Italian women were employed in sweatshops there, sewing clothes that were sold to retail stores across Canada. They worked upstairs, on the many levels of the old buildings along Spadina, north of the Queen Elizabeth Highway. Again, like immigrant men, the women were paid minimum wage, worked long hours and were often exploited. Their hard work and attention to detail made them the perfect workers. They put up with difficult working conditions in silence because they needed to work.

One such woman was Maria Di Zio, who arrived in Canada in the 1950s. She was in love with Tommaso, a farmer, whom her parents did not approve of, and because of this, the young couple married and came to Canada to begin a new life. They arrived in Timmins, Ontario, where Tommaso had been promised a well-paying, though dangerous, job in the mines. When her husband lost the opportunity to work in the mines because his employers discovered that he had health problems, Maria had to step up to the plate. She found a job sewing skating costumes for skaters at the McIntyre Arena in Timmins. In the 1950s, this was one of the only skating rinks that was open year-round, and so in the summer, Olympic skaters came to the arena to train. With the $25 that she earned for her first costume, she was able to pay the rent and to feed her family for a month. Her success is what gave Maria the incentive to continue sewing costumes and led her to start her own successful business of sewing high couture wedding dresses. Maria's entrepreneurial spirit allowed her family to thrive in their new Canadian world. And it is undoubtedly what gave her daughter Rosanna the same entrepreneurial drive with which, together with her husband Gabe, she manages their well-known Canadian Magnotta Winery in Vaughan, Ontario.

In the early 1900s, at a time when most Canadian women didn't work outside the home, Italian Canadian women worked to help support their families. They found employment in factories, in stores and as domestics. Many of them helped their husbands run fruit and grocery stores and other small businesses.

The women did all this while also taking care of their families and doing house chores. They contributed as much as the men in the family in their unfailing dream of helping their children succeed in their new country. According to Anna Makolkin, "in Canada, it took the women's movement to give women access to equal pay for equal work, while in Italy women had already achieved equality in this area. Women were already viewed as equals in a society that despite its apparent patriarchy, was and still is also very matriarchal."

In religious and social affairs, Italians have always revered women. They have been put on a pedestal, so to speak. The symbol for Italy on the old Italian lira was the image of a woman, and "Italia" is a woman's name. It is no coincidence that Mary has a high status in the Italian Catholic Church. Italy is perhaps one of the only countries where many love songs are about mothers. The "mother land" is a perfect metaphor for a country whose culture embraces womanhood as a part of itself. Italians brought this element with them to Canada. Italian immigrant women showed all along that women could do it all and succeed. Of course, their lives were filled with much hard work and sacrifice, but because of these women's efforts, immigrants were able to buy homes and provide financial stability for their children.Between the '40s and the '60s, thousands of Italian women came to Canada and brought with them their work experience, organizational skills and creative flair. In Canada in the '50s, women were not expected to go to work. It was not until the women's movement of the '60s that women entered the workforce en masse, while immigrant women were already doing so. Despite the lingering stereotype that Italian Canadian women were "old-fashioned" and kept down by their male partners, as a result of economic necessity, they were essential participants in the Canadian workforce. They were perhaps influential to other women, who seeing their success in dealing with families and work, were inspired to move out of their traditional roles in order to enter the Canadian workforce.

Anna Makolkin explains: "already by 1910, Italian women had been involved in labour unions in Italy. Italian women played a more important role in work and organizations than women did in Canada. This was probably because of a more puritanical social system." In the 1900s in Canada, women were not allowed to enter liquor stores; they were to be seen but not heard; and female teachers could not get married. Many institutions, including the medical profession, barred women from entering their exclusive male clubs. In the Italian culture, things were very different, as can be seen throughout the social fabric of Italy, in education, religion and business. For example, Maria Montessori, an elementary school teacher from southern Italy, revolutionized learning for children who were believed to be unteachable. Today, her system is used throughout Canada and the world in what we now know as the Montessori method.

Italian nuns were also influential women in Canadian life. They brought a compassionate, civilizing effect to a Canada, whose harsh climate and strict social mores did not make it a welcoming place for the early immigrants. The nuns greeted new people arriving at Pier 21 and handed out warm words of hope, toys, colouring books and crayons to the thousands of families with children arriving at Halifax.

From my own experience of landing at Pier 21, the nuns who greeted us the day we stepped off our ship into the large corridors of that Halifax station were the warmest memory I have of my first encounter on Canadian soil. In a sea of cold stares and functional passport processing by government and customs officers, nuns gave out treats and compassion to my family. They were a glimpse of hope in the otherwise growing sense of anxious foreboding for the unknown future that was about to unfold for us. Religious women were sent to Canada as missionaries with the purpose of ministering to the immigrants. They gave their lives in order to continue their humanizing and civilizing influence on our communities in the many schools, hospitals and church communities to which they ministered.

Italian women in general had an important role to play alongside Italian men in forging this country. In the periods of immigrant settlement, men brought their families with them. These women prepared meals, cleaned and took care of the men who lived in boarding houses, providing words of comfort to workers who were alone and far from home. In all families, women are the keepers of culture. They are the ones who maintain social traditions through the rituals of special holidays, meals, language and customs. Italian Canadian women were no exception. They prepared traditional meals to celebrate special religious holidays of which the most important were Christmas, the Epiphany, Carnevale, St. Joseph's Day and Easter. Women maintained communication with relatives back in Italy, through letters and telegrams, thus keeping alive the connections to their original culture for their children. Women were the ones who kept the families together.

In a book entitled *Looking Through My Mother's Eyes*, Montréal author Giovanna Del Negro writes about the importance of keeping culture alive, through the stories of nine immigrant women. Del Negro illustrates how women pass on culture to their children through the typical female rituals within the family. She focuses on the folklore of women, which is "almost any kind of physical object or social activity that has been touched and transformed by the human spirit."

It is the minutiae of women's lives that have the most profound effect on the family's culture. It is what passes on the habits and values that form cultural customs. Women's "stories of everyday life are embedded with powerful symbolic meanings, which invoke the past and become richer each time they are retold." Like my own mother's stories, which I have heard thousands of times, they are the tales that have kept Italian culture alive within the family. Everyday rituals such as food preparation, customs, stories, proverbs, songs, dances, religious celebrations and crafts become folklore when they are celebrated. Menial things become magical when people make an effort to create meaning out of them. This important task of maintaining the beauty of tradition and ritual within the family and a society is usually the domain of women.

The role of grandmothers in Italian Canadian communities is not to be discounted either. Gina Valle, writer and educator, has written much on the subject of Italian Canadian grandmothers. In her book and photo exhibit entitled "Our Grandmothers, Ourselves," she documents the importance of these women in facilitating the success of the immigrants. Grandmothers complemented the mother's role in the children's upbringing; they were also keepers of Italian culture. When mothers were busy working outside the home, grandmothers took care of the children in the family, maintaining the language and traditions. Their role as nurturers strengthened family bonds.

The women showcased in Gina Valle's "Legacies" exhibit are not two-dimensional stereotypes of immigrant women. Snapshots of real women are on display, each with unique personalities and stories. As Valle explains, "they are the gatekeepers of language and culture. They are strong, wise women, who against the unimaginable odds of war, poverty and immigration rose to the occasion of their existence to become extraordinary role models for their granddaughters." The stories are captured in print by the new generations of women who through their grandmothers' tales aim to give us "insights into the immigrant life, the changing family, feminism, intergenerational relationships and aging."

Today, Italian Canadian women are part of the Canadian social fabric. Although still tied to family and religious traditions, most Italian Canadian women work outside the home in all types of employment—writers, teachers, doctors, lawyers, engineers, actresses, playwrights, business owners, developers and CEOs of large companies. One such entrepreneurial woman is Julie Di Lorenzo, a young Italian Canadian who has earned the title of most successful developer of downtown Toronto. An article in Toronto's *Globe and Mail* states: "Di Lorenzo is probably the only woman in Canada with her kind of development

clout. She has a reputation for being a shrewd nego-
tiator, having lost money only once on an ill advised
project in California. She is a spokesperson for the
development industry, having served as the President
of the Greater Toronto Home Builders' Association
and she is a tough critic who speaks often and pub-
licly about the ad-hoc way in which the city of Toronto
is being planned." But Di Lorenzo is not alone. There
are many other women just like her who have achieved
success in every facet of Canadian life.

Italian Canadian women moved from the garment
sweatshops and harsh factory conditions to being
involved in the actual planning and building of our
cities. If their mothers worked so hard, it was to give
their daughters a better life, and indeed they succeeded.

As Rosie Di Manno, a columnist for the *Toronto Star*,
proves, Italian Canadian women today have an equal
voice in the mainstream dialogue of our nation. Some
of Canada's best women writers of Italian origin have
given a voice to the Italian community. A few names
that stand out are Mary Di Michele and Gianna Patriarca, both top female poets in the contemporary Canadian literature scene. Di Michele, who has recently
published the award-winning novel *Tenor of Love*, has
been writing award-winning poetry since the '70s.

Patriarca, through her works, has given poetic
expression to the Italian woman's experience. Some of
her collections of poetry deal with many of the issues
facing Italian immigrant women. They touch on topics
such as social isolation and dislocation caused by loss
of familial and social ties. The poems express the
angst of existing in a new world context, of feeling
different, of not being heard or seen for one's true self,

of being invisible. One of Patriarca's poems entitled "A Landscape" reads:

She looks for the landscape
In the faces she loves
They have replaced the hills
The pastures of wild margherite
The fields of red poppies...
The faces erase
The flat grey of this sky...
She has parked her soul here
For what she believed
Was a little while
And sometimes she cries
Such hard tears
For the smell of new grass
After a rainfall
The light of fireflies
On an August night
For a country that sent her away
Without asking
And imprisoned forever
A child inside the heart
Who keeps looking for landscapes
In the faces she loves

(Poem reprinted by permission of Gianna Patriarca, *Ciao Baby.* Toronto: Guernica, 1999.)

Although a recent phenomenon, writing by Italian Canadian women is a growing trend. As they rise within a variety of disciplines in the echelons of universities across the country, many Canadian women of Italian background are documenting their own experience and the experience of their mothers and grandmothers, giving a new voice to the silence that had enshrouded them for so long. An example is the recently published book of short stories by Italian Canadian women authors entitled *Mamma Mia! Good Italian Girls Talk Back!*, in which women document the idiosyncrasies of their double identities as Italian Canadians.

CBC TV host of *Canada Now,* Rita Celli, states that the book "charts the familiar, sometimes heartbreaking, often hilarious journey from childhood to adulthood, a voyage not particular to the children of Italian immigrants." These are the voices of typical women recounting stories of growing up different. According to Maria Di Cenzo, they are "reflections on pleasures and personal traumas, reminding us of how much is always at stake, for children, adults, and especially women, in navigating the complicated terrain between different cultures." Italian girls always get asked by their relatives, "When are you getting married?" In her introduction to the book, Maria Coletta McLean says: "Singledom is a state rarely accepted by Italian relatives, especially the married ones. In "Apologia for Singledom," Jennifer Febbrato establishes the hierarchy of the Italian Canadian family and discovers unmarried women like herself dangerously close to the bottom of the heap. Like many women of her generation, she opts for an education but is unable to explain her preference to her Italian-speaking grandmother. Most of their communication is mimed, and although it would be easy to tap the ring finger of the left hand to signal an engagement, Jennifer dares you to meet this challenge: 'Try miming PhD.'"

McLean, who collected all these stories from various women writers of Italian Canadian background, is also the author of the recently published book *My Father Came from Italy,* a tribute to her father's sacrifices in giving up his beautiful town of Supino in order to give his children a better economic future in Toronto. The stories she collected for *Mamma Mia!* are interesting in themselves, but the controversy that surrounded the publishing of the book is another story in itself.

Much was done by the authors themselves and by other Italians in the community to prevent the publishing of the image on the cover of the book, which depicts a woman gesticulating in a stereotypical Italian way, and has been the centre of a much heated campaign to halt this particular depiction of Italian women. Carmelina Crupi, an Italian American writer now living in Canada, declined being part of the book and told Jack David of ECW Press that "stereotypes sell, but we are not for sale." Crupi was concerned that the title of the book would infantilize Italian women, and it also contained the inherent message of talking back, which reinforces a stereotype of being unintelligent, temperamental and ill-mannered. The picture depicts a hot-headed woman engaging in cliché behaviour.

Writer Gina Valle has stated that it was hardly the look for a reputable literary work. "It's just a silly book cover and title. It's just senseless marketing. It's just one book," Valle was told by the publishers, "but I would argue otherwise" says Valle. "It is because we live in a multicultural country that we need to find practical ways in which to ensure that all citizens, and all members of ethno-cultural communities, are able to live full lives, free of restrictive stereotypes. An effective way in which to ensure that all citizens, no matter their origins, can participate in all aspects of their lives is to be vigilant of stereotype when it occurs."

Gina Valle's work aims to teach Canadians the importance of the eradication of stereotype. It is an insidious problem that deteriorates the quality of life and the self-concept of many communities, hampering the full expression of their innate potential. Valle is one Italian Canadian woman whose work is helping Canadians to grow toward a potentially freer future, where stereotypes will one day be the relics of ancient history.

In our multicultural mosaic, the voices of these Italian women contain a message of hope for all other women entering the country today. The message is one of staying grounded in one's own identity and values, yet embracing the new in a state of constant open-mindedness. Italian Canadian women have demonstrated that through hard work, self-discipline, perseverance and a strong sense of family and community, successful futures can become a reality.

CHAPTER EIGHT

DEMOGRAPHICS

The edges of inhabitation are distinct…
A hundred, two hundred
A thousand more and more
We inhabit the foreign, we are the foreign.

—Pasquale Verdicchio

In a radio interview in May 2007, Toni Gagliano, the publisher of Toronto *Life* magazine told a CBC reporter of the $10 million gift donated by the Italian community of Toronto to the Art Gallery of Ontario, which through such funding will open a new wing named *The Galleria Italia* in the spring of 2008. Initially Gagliano's idea, he was able to garner the support of Hilary Weston, Michael Lee Chin, Dominic D'Alessandro and Fred De Gasparis, who embraced the concept. They rounded up families from the Italian Canadian community who all together donated the $10 million. It was their way of making a contribution to the arts in Toronto. Gagliano explained in the interview that the hard-working Italian immigrant mentality is a reflection of their Italian ancestry. Today's Italian Canadians are trying to create a strong bond between Italy and Canada through the arts. Gagliano is proud that the Italians had such a strong role in kicking off multiculturalism in Canada. They are paying back the two countries they love the most—Canada and Italy—by giving the Art Gallery of Ontario a name that reflects their old country, one that contributed so much to the arts over the millennia. More than anything, this generous gift by the Italian Canadians is only one of many gestures on their part of wanting to give back to Canada, the country that has given them so much. Moreover, Gagliano believes that the Italians' donation is also a sign of their newfound success and prosperity.

Italian Canadians are no longer the new immigrants. They no longer struggle to make ends meet. The children of the second wave immigrants are now an integral part of the new face of Canada. They are involved in the political decision-making and the financial, academic, artistic and cultural make-up of their communities. In the 2001 census, 1,270,370 people claimed to have Italian ancestry in Canada. Of these, 726,275 had purely Italian origins. The rest, 544,090, were partly of Italian origin. Italian Canadians make up 4.3 percent of the population of Canada, the majority of whom live in Ontario. There are 781,345 Italian Canadians living there, and they make up seven percent of the population. Another 249,205 Italians live in the province of Québec, with the remainder of them spread out throughout the other provinces. These numbers make them the largest number of Italians living outside the boundaries of Italy. All together, they are almost a country outside of their own homeland.

From the census taken in 2001, the Italian composition per province in Canada was as follows.

ITALIAN CANADIANS BY PROVINCE AND TERRITORY (PERCENT OF POPULATION):

Ontario 781,345 (6.9 percent)
Québec 249,205 (3.5 percent)
British Columbia 126,420 (3.3 percent)
Alberta 67,655 (2.3 percent)
Manitoba 18,550 (1.7 percent)
Nova Scotia 11,240 (1.3 percent)
Saskatchewan 7569 (0.8 percent)
New Brunswick 5610 (0.8 percent)
Newfoundland and Labrador 1180 (0.2 percent)
Prince Edward Island 605 (0.5 percent)
Yukon 500 (1.8 percent)
Northwest Territories 400 (1.1 percent)
Nunavut 95 (0.4 percent)

According to the 2001 census, the main concentrations of Italian Canadians are in the metropolitan areas, although many Italian Canadians reside in smaller centres: 429,380 in the greater Toronto area; 224,460 in the Montréal area; 69,000 in Vancouver; 67,685 in Hamilton; 44,645 in the St. Catherines-Niagara area; 37,435 in Ottawa-Hull; 30,680 in Windsor, Ontario; 29,120 in the Calgary region; 16,315 in Sault Ste. Marie, Ontario; 15,395 in Thunder Bay, Ontario; 13,990 in Oshawa, Ontario; 12,030 in Sudbury, Ontario; and 11,135 in Guelph, Ontario.

The 2001 census indicates that three-quarters of Italian Canadians were born in Canada. The remaining one-quarter were immigrants, born in Italy. This portion of Italian-born Canadian residents came to Canada before 1961 and another 10 percent of them between 1971 and 1980. After 1980, Italian immigration to Canada has been almost nonexistent. Since 1981, a meagre 6.4 percent of Italian immigrants chose to come to Canadian cities.

More than half of Italian Canadians speak English as their first language. The rest, according to the census, speak French. Of the 1.3 million Italians living in Canada, 469,485 speak Italian. This is a large number, considering that Italian is not taught in all schools throughout the country.

As far as religion, most Italian Canadians in 2001 belonged to the Catholic faith. Of the 1.3 million, 1,015,725 were Roman Catholic. Due to intermarriage or other factors, 113,455 were Protestant. The rest— 23,805—were other than Christian. Atheists constituted 109,515 people. The largest non-Christian religious group that some Italians followed was Judaism.

In 2001, Italian Canadians had above-average incomes compared to other Canadians, earning an average yearly income of $34,871 compared to the national average of $31,757. They had below-average unemployment rates compared to other Canadians as a whole. Unemployed Italian Canadians represented 5.4 percent of the population, while other Canadians stood at 7.4 percent of the unemployed labour force. Still, in 2001, Italian Canadians were shown to be disproportionately employed as construction workers. Six percent of people employed in construction work are Italian Canadian. Of course, work in all other walks of life and the Italian Canadian presence in other industries is about equal to the general Canadian population.

In the 1981 census, it was observed that Italian Canadians had lower than national average levels of education. After World War II, many Italian immigrants in Canada had low levels of education, because they came from rural areas. When they arrived in Canada, their main concern was finding work in order to sustain their families; furthering their education was not a priority. As late as 1971, 56 percent of Italian Canadian children had completed grade nine or less as compared to the national average of 25 percent. Many teachers and school administrators believed that Italian immigrants didn't want higher education for their children. The result was that many high school students of Italian origin were channelled toward vocational careers. They did not go to universities or colleges, because their parents were not highly educated themselves, could not speak the language, could not help them with homework and could not communicate with their children's teachers.

Two and a half decades later, things look different. In the 2001 Canadian census, students of Italian origin began to resemble the national average of young people attending community colleges and universities. Today, Canadians of Italian origin are as likely as other Canadians to pursue higher education. For the younger generations, who were born in Canada and had parents who were either born here or have lived here for decades, life is a lot different than it was for the first immigrants.

Outside central Canada, Vancouver became the most popular destination for Italian immigrants. In

1941 the city was home to 4359 Italians, but by 1981, immigration had increased the number of Italian Canadians in Vancouver to over 30,000. Winnipeg, Calgary and Edmonton also witnessed a rise in the Italian population during the 1950s. Edmonton attracted large numbers of labourers, the first significant group arriving in 1954 with the R.F. Welch Company. Between 1951 and 1961 the Italian community in Edmonton went from 500 inhabitants to 4425. A decade later it rose to 10,000.

One of the Italian immigrants living in Alberta was one of my father's friends, Armando Perfetti. He was among the thousands of workers who made their way from their Italian hometowns in the 1960s to the barren, snow-covered prairies of the West, looking for success. When I was a child, I remember my father's joy at receiving an airmail letter, the kind with the blue, white and red stripes on the edges, from his friend Armando. Schoolmates and teenage friends, my father and "Armandino," as he was affectionately nicknamed, had shared their youth and dreams together. The photograph inside the letter was of Armando, dressed in winter clothing, squatting down by a railway track and squinting a smile for the camera. What was most striking in the photo was the contrast of his dark clothing against the total whiteness of the snow-covered background, interrupted by the black steel of the train tracks. From Edmonton, with love and friendship, Armando had brought a tear to my father's eye, who at this point hadn't even thought of emigrating to Canada.

Some of my father's friends headed mostly for Edmonton, a resource-based town that attracted many immigrants. Spread throughout the country,

Miners in Sudbury (1922).

Italians settled in the city of Trail in British Columbia, and the cities of Sudbury and Sault Ste. Marie in Ontario. Chain migration resulted in the large numbers of post-war Italians settling in Sault Ste. Marie, so that by the 1960s, the Italian ethnic group emerged as the town's second largest. In 1971 they numbered over 13,000, the highest proportion of Italians anywhere in Canada.

The Aluminum Company of Canada hired 430 Italians in the aluminum-producing town of Kitimat in British Columbia; another 300 of them were employed in the nickel-mining town of Thompson, Manitoba, by the International Nickel Company. Hundreds of other Italians were attracted to the copper and gold mines in the Rouyn area of northeastern Québec, and roughly

200 of them lived in Yellowknife, in the Northwest Territories, where gold mining provided employment.

By the 1970s, the Italians in the major metropolitan areas of Toronto and Montréal began to move out from the city core to the suburbs, where they created new Italian Canadian communities. In Toronto, most Italians moved to the area of Woodbridge, while in Montréal it was Saint-Leonard.

According to Robert Harney:

Riding the crest of economic prosperity, Toronto's Italians continued to push their urban advance to the northwest at a rapid pace, attesting to the group's drive to attain a middle-class standard of living. Through the suburban communities of York and North York, Italians moved toward the metropolitan limits, where by the 1970s they formed up to half the population in neighbourhoods such as Downsview. From there, they shifted outside Metropolitan Toronto altogether, to adjacent towns such as Woodbridge, which because of its high concentration of the second generation, Italianate-architecture, and various Italian Canadian businesses has come to symbolize most vividly, the mobility of Italian Canadians in the nation's major urban areas.

Census figures reveal that Italian Canadians made major strides in upward mobility during the 1970s and 1980s. In the 15-year period between 1971 and 1986, they increased their proportion in the nation's managerial, professional and technical occupations, from 7 to over 17 percent, and in clerical, sales and service jobs from 31 to over 41 percent. Conversely, the proportion of Italian Canadians in blue-collar work, such as manufacturing, construction and transportation, dropped from 60 to 40 percent. In 1986, about one-quarter of Canadian-educated men and women were in managerial, professional and technical occupations, compared to a small proportion of around six percent for the immigrant generation. Canadian-educated Italian males had virtually reached parity with Canadians generally, but females were five percent below their counterparts. Within the upper level category, the most prominent profession for Italian Canadian men and women was management and administration, which accounted for 12 percent of the total for men and eight percent for women.

White-collar jobs in clerical, sales and service accounted for almost 35 percent of Canadian-educated Italian males and 69 percent of females, higher than the 26 and 59 percent of the general population. In blue-collar occupations, 38 percent of Canadian-educated Italian men and almost seven percent of women were in this category, close to the overall Canadian proportions. There was a remarkable decrease of 43 percent in the proportion of Italian women engaged in manual labour within the span of one generation.

The profile depicted by these statistics is indicative of the Italians' educational attainment. In 1986 over 12 percent of male and 10 percent of female children of Italian immigrants had received a bachelor of arts degree or higher. For boys, this ratio was identical to the national average, whereas for girls it was slightly higher by two percent. The attainment of higher education improved the employment options of Italian Canadians.

With regard to income, another major indicator of socio-economic status, the general level reached by

Italian Canadians in 1986 was equivalent to the mainstream Canadian average income of almost $15,000. By the 1980s many immigrant men were at the height of their earning power, while their sons were still establishing themselves. Daughters were entering white-collar careers, which was in contrast to the intermittent factory work that employed their mothers. In cities like Toronto, the income of men of Italian origin was higher for the self-employed but also for people who worked in Italian businesses and traditional Italian occupations. Many immigrant entrepreneurs who had set up their own small businesses, especially in the construction and food industries, prospered in the post-war boom and became major employers, providing jobs to large numbers of other Italians. The size of the city's Italian population, which accounted for 37 percent of the nation's total, enabled the community to develop an ethnically based economy that far from acting as a barrier to upward mobility, often enhanced it.

Italian Canadians experienced impressive upward mobility in the post-war era when looking at the occupation, education and income. Significant intergenerational improvement was made, and rough parity with mainstream Canadians was attained in the 1980s. The most important facet of success for Italian Canadians, however, must be taken into consideration, and this was home ownership. Being able to have their own home was most cherished, and it reflected both the wish to own land, which was so scarce in Italy, and the values they attached to family and hearth. It is undoubtedly because of these reasons that by the 1980s, Italians had attained the highest rate of home ownership in Canada. In 1981,

86 percent of Italians owned homes, well above the national average of 70 percent. And 37 percent owned homes worth more than $100,000, compared to 22 percent of other Canadians.

Italian immigrants have definitely succeeded in improving their own and their children's lives. The major socio-economic indicators demonstrate that Italian Canadians today are firmly rooted in the middle-class mainstream of Canada.

CHAPTER NINE

PRESENZA: HOW THE ITALIAN PRESENCE CONTRIBUTED TO LIFE IN CANADA

In order to realize who they were, they needed to know where they came from, and why and how they were here, to make it clear both to themselves as well as to other fellow Canadians.
–From "The Virtual Piazza" by Monica Stellin

I n 2003, the Canadian Museum of Civilization in Ottawa honoured Italian Canadians with the first-ever exhibit on the heritage and day-to-day lives of Italian Canadians. The exhibition looked at the values, skills and traditions that a generation of Italian immigrants brought to Canada and showed how relevant they have been for generations of Canadians. It attempted to define to Italian Canadians themselves, and to the rest of Canada, the relevance of Italian immigrants and how their presence has impacted Canadian culture. "Presenza" was an exhibit designed to present a series of scenes showing artifacts, video-taped interviews and fictional characters re-enacting dramas and situations or encounters between Italian Canadians and their fellow citizens.

The museum's introductory message about their exhibit of Italian Canadian heritage was as follows.

Italian Canadians: they live among us—our fellow citizens, neighbours and friends. But the roots of their communities lie with the people who one day decided to leave the places where they were born and raised: the immigrants. They came mainly from rural Italy, and brought in their suitcases traditions and values from their peasant societies they left behind. Their outlook, way of life, knowledge and know-how are now an integral part of the Canadian fabric. This exhibition is about their presence.

The museum gathered 300 artifacts from across Canada. Many of the personal objects were loaned by individuals, ranging from accordions to family photos to wedding dresses. Other objects in the exhibit included everyday items such as cutlery, dinnerware, linens, folk art, regional artifacts and even a restored FIAT automobile. The objects included in the exhibit all had a part in expressing the meaning of Italian culture. From some of their original suitcases, complete with actual documents, photos, passports and clothing, we get a time-capsule view of how their immigration voyage unfolded.

The most interesting part of the exhibit was the re-creation of a central square, or *piazza*. No Italian town is without at least one piazza, the focal point of societal, civil interaction. It has been perhaps the one aspect of Italian life that immigrants have missed most, the heart of Italian cities, where people prome-nade in style, sit at their cafés reading, sipping espresso or licking their hazelnut-lemon gelato, enjoy-ing the view of fountains and historical sites. The piazza was the site of feasts and open markets for thousands of years in Italian life. It was the meeting place for spiritual worship as well, as churches were usually built at one corner of the central square, with its main doors looking out. Body, mind and spirit were all nourished in one place. Political discourse, the arts, literature, philosophy, science and fashion trends all had their beginnings in the tight-knit human interactions of people congregating in piazzas. In Pre-senza, all the details, from fountains to cobblestone streets, to typical trees and cityscapes were recreated to give the museum-goers a facsimile of what a true piazza is truly like.

On the same vein was the exhibit's focus on Italian community spaces commonly found in Italian villages. Unlike Canadian cities, with their grids of wide streets and boulevards, where business is conducted swiftly, Italian towns were usually perched at the top of hills ribboned with small roads and paths of stairs. People didn't hurry there, and they took the time to chat with one another and to watch their children play. Life took precedence over work, therefore business activities would often be interrupted by religious celebrations and other celebrations pertaining to the harvest. This slowing down of life in order to enjoy the little things is one aspect of Italian culture that immigrants brought with them and which Presenza tried to cap-ture in their re-creation of an exhibit titled "The Roots of a Community." The museum's introduction to the exhibit states: "perhaps their cafés and patios, the parks where they play bocce and the neighbourhoods through which their processions travel are ways of recreating the sinewy lanes of their villages. Perhaps this is a clever means of getting us to slow down and be patient, of inviting us to take the time to talk to people, to listen to them and perhaps weave the roots of a community."

Italians are social people and love congregating with others. Many of them remember how in the 1950s, groups of Italians who gathered on the sidewalks in Canada to chat were often dispersed by the police, accused of loitering, with imagined suspicions of their assumed criminality. Imagine the surprise of these newcomers, who were simply doing what they always had done back home: chat in the piazza, take a stroll (*una passeggiata*) or play cards with their friends at a sidewalk café. Interestingly, since then, Canadians have adopted the Italian way of doing things. Cafés, patios and sidewalks are filled with people who chat and stroll while eating ice cream in cities all over Canada. The urban scene of many Canadian cities is now reminiscent of Italy, and this is due to the cultural contribution made by Italian Canadians.

One of the oil paintings hanging in the art exhibit of Presenza, by canvas artist Salvatore Zilembo, depicts a peasant sitting in his garden drinking wine and eating some of his plentiful harvest, in an earthly paradise background view. The painting is aptly called *Il Contadino* (The Peasant), and for the artist it depicts more than a peasant taking a break at harvest time. Based on his childhood memories, it also captures the pleasure of living close to nature, and the peasant's love for his land and its produce. Photos, paintings and other media in the Ottawa exhibit gathered all of the vegetables, legumes, aromatic plants, herbs and fruits cultivated by Italians, which through their immigration all made their way to Canada.

When it comes to fruit trees, nothing stirs the nostalgia of Italians like the fig tree. Even though the fig tree can't withstand the cold temperatures of Canadian winters, most Italians successfully grow them in their backyards. At the end of summer, fig trees in Canadian gardens are laden with fruit, although perhaps not as large or sweet as the ones in Italy, but with a fleshy, delicious taste nonetheless. If you have ever wondered how these Mediterranean trees can withstand our harsh winters, Presenza shows you how these precious, yet delicate fruit trees can grow in Canadian gardens. Italians have been using a simple procedure, one that stems from the desire to enjoy a fig at any cost, since their arrival in Canada. The branches of the fig tree are bound with rope to prevent them from spreading. Then a trench is dug, which should be the length of the whole tree. The fig tree is then uprooted halfway and lowered into the trench, at which point the tree is covered over with soil, leaves and even wood or plastic in order to insulate the tree from the icy winter. In the spring, the tree is dug up and raised up again, with its roots firmly replanted. At the end of the summer, the perfectly healthy fig tree should yield many delicious figs, and figs to Italians are like the nectar of the Gods. I have seen many a fig tree in Italian gardens. The biggest one I have ever seen made me stop the car and gasp in amazement. It was planted in a garage, which had been converted into a glass greenhouse and whose floor, which was not visible from the road, must have been dug up in order to plant the tree. What wild and crazy things Italians wouldn't do for a fig tree!

In the section of Presenza aptly entitled *Knowing What to Eat*, the museum organizers also display the tools used to cultivate different types of produce. Carlo Ferrera, for example, lent a tree pruning knife that he brought with him from Lazio in the 1960s. Made of metal and wood, the knife was used to prune fruit trees or to cut firewood. In Canada, Ferrera uses the knife to prune the trees in his garden. The curved inner edge is for cutting narrow branches, and the outer edge serves as a hatchet, for cutting large branches or trunks. Other garden tools include pruning shears, also from Lazio, lent to the exhibit by Orazio Di Cocco; and an axe and pruning shears from Sicily, brought to Canada by Salvatore Valenti in 1948. Valenti pruned olive trees in Italy. Thinking that these shears might come in handy, he brought them to Canada, where he continued to use them in his garden.

Other garden items on display were a brush clearing tool made of metal and wood and a sickle brought by Pompilio Rocca in the 1930s; another sickle made by Salvatore Lamonica in Canada, in 1962; and a vine-grafting knife, made by Carmine Michele Zilembo in Molise, in the 1950s. It was made of metal and a goat horn and was used to graft one type of fruit tree into the trunk of another fruit tree, thus creating a new type of fruit. Fruit tree grafting was a technique that Italians passed on from generation to generation of fruit growers and it influenced fruit production in Canadian farms.

In the *Knowing What to Eat* section of Presenza, we also find the special machines that Italians imported to Canada in order to prepare some of their specialty fare. Among the main items is an electric grape crusher made in Canada in 1964 by Sebastiano Sgromo, who arrived in Thunder Bay in 1957. Unable to find the equipment he needed to make wine, he drew upon his metalworking skills to design and build an electric grape crusher. He still uses it every year and lends it to relatives and friends, who take turns with it in the fall when it's time to make wine. A manual grape press, similar to the kind in most Italian Canadian homes, was lent by Antonio Giancarlo. The press was built in Canada in the 1920s and is made of wood and metal. Other items pertaining to winemaking are wine barrel faucets made by Tobia Landero in Canada (circa 1960) and lent by Tobia and Ivana Londero. The Londeros also donated a bottle corker used to seal wine bottles.

Another machine on display is a red, metal, commercial sausage stuffer. This particular item comes from England and was made around 1900. It was lent to the exhibit by Rocky Giovinazzo of Rocky's Meats in Vancouver. Rocco Giovinazzo worked in several butcher shops before opening Rocky's Meats with his wife Silvia, in 1961. It was one of the first butcher shops in Vancouver to produce Italian sausages. Convinced that food prepared using traditional methods tasted better, Mr. Giovinazzo kept this manual sausage stuffer until he sold his shop in 1999. Not everyone had a large, electric sausagemaker like this one, however, so on display are other sausage-making machines that families would have in their homes. A domestic sausage stuffer from Molise dates back from the 1940s and was donated by Carmelina Corsi Cusano. A meat grinder made in 1900 in Italy was lent by Arduino Dino Rossi. Finally, a metal and wood meat cleaver, made in Italy and of unknown date of manufacture, was lent by Vilma Ricci. Of course, the various types of stuffed meats, from sausages, capi-collo, soppressata, prosciutto and cotechino are all mentioned and displayed in the foods exhibit.

Because cheese-making was another Italian custom, on top of images and lists of the different kinds of cheeses Italians introduced to Italian cuisine, we find ricotta cheese drainers, mozzarella cheese moulds, ricotta cheese spoons and curd ladles from Calabria, Abruzzo and Sicily, ranging from the 1920s to the 1970s.

Unlocking the Past is one of the titles of Presenza. The history and diversity of the people who arrived in Canada from Italy is viewed through the videotaped recordings of real people telling their families' stories, replete as they were with concerns, hopes and dreams. Every person's story is different; every case unique. Each immigrant has pursued his or her own path, depending on factors such as education, risk taking and aspirations. Through all of their different stories, however, runs the common thread of identity and values, which distinguished their contribution to the making of Canada.

It is said that a picture is worth a thousand words. In Presenza, the museum tried to sum up a million Italian Canadians through the iconography of their objects. Through their artifacts we can begin to understand the Italian way of life and how it contributed to Canada: their passion for beauty and art; their appreciation for family gatherings and meals; their love of cafés, espresso and gelato; their attention to detail and design; their love of soccer and beautiful cars; their customs and family strength.

But how did the Italian presence really influence our way of life in Canada?

The exhibit tried to show how the meeting of cultures changed the way we actually live our everyday lives. From 1880 to 1970, several hundred thousand Italians came to Canada. They formed one of the most visible communities in Canada's cities. Their lifestyle became renowned and coveted. They had strong family and community ties. Their home production of food and wine and their celebrations were admired by all. Their traditions and skills were of value to their own families and cultural groups, but they also spilled over into their adoptive culture.

In today's fast-paced, technological, impersonal world, Italian Canadian values are important. They speak of appreciation for slow-paced detail; appreciation for beauty, art and friendship; celebration of family and life. Their values are relevant today to address many social problems. They are also reflected in the new Canadian way of doing things that has changed, partly because the Italians were here. From healthy eating to the new search for community in espresso bars, which are the new rage, to the appreciation for Italian fashion, Italian culture has changed the face and feeling of public space in Canadian cities.

Vegetable gardens, for example, were not a hot item in Canada's gardening scene before the Italians arrived. Today it has become fashionable to grow vegetables alongside the tea roses and lavender of Canadian English gardens. This change is typical of the subtle, yet profound changes brought into the Canadian culture by the Italian presence. Who would have ever thought of growing basil or arugula in their gardens before the Italians? Arugula, an unusual bittersweet plant that was once unknown here, is now the staple of every gourmet salad repertoire. And so it goes for every other type of vegetable that was once the staple of Italian culture, and has now made it to the front cover of the best Canadian cookbooks. What vegetables and herbs did Italians bring to Canada? Here is a comprehensive list taken from Presenza's collection:

Arugula	Zucchini	Rosemary
Cabbage	Beans (fagioli)	Sage
Carrots	Fava beans	Tarragon
Celery	Green beans	Thyme
Eggplant	Basil	Apples
Lettuce:	Bay	Figs
scarola,	Fennel	Grapes
romana,	Hot peppers	Plums
radicchio	Mint	Tomatoes
Onions	Oregano	
Peppers	Parsley	

Of course, some of these plants and vegetables were already used in Canada, but it was the variety and the way in which they were used that gave them a particular new flavour. Italians grew many of these fruits, vegetables and herbs in their backyards. This practice was later adopted by other Canadians, who saw the benefit of growing their own food. Today, gardening is considered a trendy hobby and is the stuff of Canada's best gardening magazines.

Italian farmers bringing a successful harvest to market.

My mother loves her garden. In the summer she spends most of her time watering and tending to her tomato plants, coddling them and worrying about strong winds or hail storms that could damage her small but precious harvest. So it is too for all other first-generation Italian Canadians. In the summer, they work in their gardens of basil, parsley, tomatoes, radicchio and zucchini. They trim grape vines; tend to fig, peach, pear and plum trees. They do so with zest and purpose, as if they were still harvesting for survival. When I go to my mother's garden, in a way I am revisiting Italy. Her patio is decorated with large terracotta pots filled with pink and white oleanders. Parsley, rosemary, oregano and bright red, hot peppers overflow from smaller pots. The grape vines my father planted 20 years ago are now thriving, with large green leaves and purple fruit in the fall. Beyond the well-manicured fruit trees, my mother's vegetable garden is a paradise of the sweetest Italian delicacies. I never leave her place without gifts of fragrant basil, oregano, parsley, onions and, of course, tomatoes, peppers, eggplants, flat green beans, cucumbers and zucchini.

In the summer I am a gourmet cook just like my mother. Those are the days of minestrone, peperonata (a sort of Italian ratatouille) and fritto misto, enjoyed on the patio to the sounds of Italian music from CHIN radio, along with a glass of my mother's homemade wine, which she still makes religiously every year, as if my father were still here. It is her way of keeping him alive, of keeping the ritual of her life alive, every detail of it, the synchronized heartbeat of her exis-tence. Perhaps harvesting and preparing these vege-tables is not an act of physical survival anymore, but it is what ties Italians to the earth they now call home, as if in growing these familiar plants they can tran-scend time and space back to the land they carry in their souls, this new garden, the illusion of the old one, giving them a common reference to the new place they now inhabit. Growing an Italian garden makes them feel as if they are still in Italy, in their childhood gardens, at home.

The same can be said for food preparation and wine making. The interest in making homemade wine by the general public is unprecedented. It is the reason why wine companies such as Vin Bon and Magnotta, do so well in the sector of their companies that deals with make–it-yourself wine kits of all sorts. When my father bought sweet California grapes from some of the Italian corner stores where he shopped, the fall winemaking was something that only our family and the families of all my other Italian friends did. It was quite the event, with friends and uncles dropping by to check out the quality of the grapes, to help out with the wine press, to help fill the barrels and, of course, to make predictions on the successfulness of the finished product at the time of fermentation. The aroma is indelibly etched in my memories of Canadian falls at my parents' house. It was in the early '70s, and it was a ritual that only Italians observed. My non-Italian friends would always look on in amazement at the amount of work and mess that was required to make wine, when their parents just went to buy some at the liquor store. What used to cause me so much embarrassment has now caught on as a trend within the general public and become quite the market within the Canadian wine business. It was because of people like my father that ideas such as making homemade wine caught everyone else's imagination.

Canada has the largest selection of breads, cheeses, meat products and wines in the world. And because of our large multi-ethnic population, we have a wide variety of food products coming into our country from every part of the globe. Italian foods, however, remain at the top of the list. Their simplicity and goodness have now become a staple of our Canadian way of life. The Italian foods found in supermarkets today used to be the simple items of Italian people's meals. Just a few decades ago, if you wanted to sample these foods you had to go either to a small Italian specialty grocery store or to an Italian home. Some common deli meats and cheeses brought into Canadian culture by Italians are:

Prosciutto (dried ham)
Capicollo (pork loin sausage)

Soppressata (ham sausage)
Pancetta (lean bacon)
Cotechino (spicy pork sausage)
Salsiccia di fegato (liver sausage)
Ricotta cheese (whey cheese)
Parmigiano
Mozzarella
Provolone
Bocconcini
Caciocavallo
Formaggio Casalingo (homemade cow's milk cheese)

Of course, other Italian foods have become staples of Canadian cooking—pasta and pizza being the main ones. Even cookies, such as ladyfingers, amaretti and almond biscotti, are no longer distinguishable as purely Italian staples. The same can be said for Tiramisu, gelato and espresso.

The presence of Italian people in Canada has left a cultural imprint on the country. Not liking to be solitary individuals, Italians chose to live in communities where relatives and other people from their town or region also lived. They helped each other out with employment and housing. They formed clubs and associations, and such groups continue to express Italian Canadian community life across the country. One of the most well-known cultural hubs of the Italian community in Toronto is the Columbus Centre. There are thousands of other such clubs in towns and cities all throughout Canada, though on a smaller scale.

Even in Oakville, where my mother lives, there is a sort of Little Italy. The neighbourhood where she lives was built in the 1950s to provide housing to the thousands of Italian labourers that were hired in the Oakville area by the Ford Motor Company's largest Southern Ontario automobile and truck plant.

Many were hired on at Saint Lawrence Cement at the outskirts of town to the south, while others found work in the many flourishing manufacturing factories sprouting around the Oakville service roads in the '50s and '60s, such as General Electric and Canadian Plastics. Many Italian women worked in these companies, making light bulbs and appliances and manufacturing plastic items on assembly lines that rewarded piece work and overtime hours with extra pay.

Many Italian labourers were also hired by the two refineries that bordered the town of Oakville, BP to the southeast of it and Shell to the west. Upon his arrival to Canada in 1968, my father was hired by Shell Refinery.

In those days, before the intense development sprawl of subdivisions, Oakville was the small area between Trafalgar Road and Lakeshore to the east, and Third Line and Lakeshore to the west. Beyond Third Line was the small town of Bronte, a picturesque cottage town of small, white and baby blue siding houses, with tugboats and small sailboats along its pier. My dad used to drive us there for ice cream. There was no gelateria in Bronte, of course. The best ice cream was available at a small variety store along the old strip of stores and houses that have since been demolished and redeveloped into condos. The refinery was outside of Bronte, north of Mississaga Street and what was then a dirt road shooting off New Street, in the acres of forested lands below the Queen Elizabeth Highway. In the 1960s no developments could be foreseen here, but today, the refinery that was bought out by Petro Canada in the 1970s is being knocked down due to relocation out west. The old Shell lands surrounding the refinery area are built up with new subdivisions all the way down to the lakefront.

My family bought a bungalow in central Oakville, in a subdivision that as I found out much later was built in the late 1950s to accommodate a burgeoning Italian immigrant population. The Italians were so numerous in Oakville at that time that an Italian priest was requested by the local bishop in order to start up a church that would meet the spiritual and community needs of so many people. It was in the '50s that Father Augusto Pucci arrived in Oakville, the town he would grow to love and call home. A high school physics and chemistry teacher in his city of Torino, Father Pucci came to Canada to minister to the thousands of Italians who were called to work in Oakville. Excited and happy by the prospect of having their own parish, the Italians collected money and recruited workers to build St. James Church, on Morden Road, just north of Rebecca Street. With its characteristic '60s architecture, the church's roof is reminiscent of an airplane taking off. How befitting of a church of people aspiring to spirituality, but also aspiring to the dream of one day flying home. Always flying home is what our dream was, but like the sturdy bricks of the church, stuck as it was in its Canadian foundations, we never did. Nobody did. We stayed.

My father died at Shell Refinery one evening, at the age of 46, of congestive heart failure. He was buried at Trafalgar Lawn Cemetery, on Highway 5. My mother, my sister and I settled in Oakville. We took our Canadian citizenship. We worked, went to school and made ourselves a life here, but Italy remained the dream of who we were, once. The church is such a great metaphor for the Italian immigrant. Like St. James church, we look as if we are always ready to fly off, but we stay put.

Father Pucci also stayed put and was influential in the Italian community. He organized committees for men and women. He set up prayer groups, healing groups, craft afternoons for the women, spaghetti dinners, picnics, baseball games, trips to Midland and Niagara Falls, bazaars, fundraising dances and youth groups. When I was in high school, I joined his Italian choir, for which he played the organ, while the kids would sing. He was always patient and kind, always present and punctual. He helped so many people with translations and paper work. He bailed people out of legal problems, mediated and advocated on their behalf with courts and employers. He helped people find jobs and took care of them when tragedy struck.

When my father died, Father Pucci came to our home the week before Thanksgiving with a box full of food for us. Inside the box was a giant turkey and all kinds of other treats, which he had packed up for our dinner. My mother was touched by his gesture. A man of few words, Father Pucci had a big heart. Even though he is in his 90s now, he still says the Italian mass every Sunday morning, to an aging Italian congregation. He has tried moving to South America and to the United States, called there by other missions, but he always returns to Oakville. He told the congregation one day that the city is his home. The Italians built him a church and a house here. This is where he belongs. And that's encouraging for the older members of the community, who in their lifelong struggle for identity and search for a place to call home, like Father Pucci, have made their home in Oakville.

Italians get attached to people. They are communal and love to interact socially with others. In Italy this was fostered and facilitated by people's life in a *paese* (town). It is because of this quality that Italians seek out kindred friends with whom to share conversations and celebrations. Many Italian Canadian clubs reflect this phenomenon. They are not Italian national clubs but are regional and reflect the diversity of Italians living in our country. Hundreds of hometown associations bring together people from the same Italian towns. People from the same villages or regions as well as national associations co-exist in many communities. These clubs give Italian Canadians a place where they can meet and share a common language, common beliefs and a sense of belonging.

Perhaps some of the most influential associations for the Italian Canadian community were Italian newspaper presses at the beginning of the 20th century. They were followed in the early '60s by radio and television stations that offered programming in Italian to immigrants. These developments contributed to a cohesiveness of the Italian Canadian community, giving them a rich and complex "Italianita" that is uniquely Canadian. In the last few years local radio and television stations have started to include programming directly from Italy, via satellite.

From the coast of Newfoundland and Labrador to the shores of Vancouver Island, Italians have lived, worked and integrated into their host communities. They have done so through work and intermarriage. No longer relegated to the physical jobs of their early immigration, they are businesspeople, politicians, professors, designers, tailors, dressmakers, ranch owners, hockey players, writers, poets, painters, geologists, graphic artists, actors, dancers, and more. To their own particular endeavours they bring a certain ethos of warmth and passion. They hold in their ethos a sense of communion with the other. In their hearts and souls there is an echo of family, community and a taste for life that is uniquely Italian.

Canada is a cosmopolitan country. With the great influx of immigrants from every part of the world, the flavour of our communities is multicultural. The Italian cultural imprint, however, is still strongly felt. Cafés and espresso bars are all the vogue nowadays. Italian words for coffee, milk and all other java concoctions are part of our common language. Italian restaurants are mainstream. So, too, are Italian recipes of all sorts, from veal scaloppini to bruschetta.

From food to beverages to design, art and media, Italian culture has permeated every aspect of our lives. Film director Francis Ford Coppola has said: "All of a sudden, there are great Japanese films, great Italian films or great Australian films. It's usually because there are a number of people that cross pollinate each other." Canadians of every ethnicity have pollinated each other. The Italian presence has left its unique imprint on Canadian culture, leaving it different than it had been before the Italians arrived.

CHAPTER TEN

LITTLE ITALYS: CHANGING THE FLAVOUR OF CANADIAN CITIES

*The best part was the food. There are some great
Italian restaurants we go to whenever we
are in Toronto, so eating is a definite highlight.*
–Mary Kate Olsen's comment upon visiting the city of
Toronto for one of her films

On a typical Saturday evening in the summer, crowds of fashionably dressed youth stroll along the sidewalks of Toronto's Little Italy. They come from all over the city and from the suburbs. They are not all Italian, but they are lured to this magical spot by the ambiance. You can see people sitting at outdoor café patios, sipping their cappuccino or cold glass of white Valpolicella. Some are relishing a creamy cone of gelato alla panna, while others are revelling in the Italian art of people watching. As night falls, the garlands of mini-lights decorating the trees along the street begin to twinkle like blue fire-flies, as blue as the little boot of Italy attached to every lamp post. An Italian song plays in the background. From elsewhere a Latin rhythm. The aroma of espresso fills the air. Welcome to Toronto's Little Italy!

Although unique in some aspects, the Little Italy in Toronto could be the setting of any other Canadian or American city. You could be in Vancouver or Ottawa or Montréal or Brooklyn's Piccola Italia. From the name itself we intuitively know why these neighbour-hoods exist. Italians living abroad try to recreate their old world setting, although on a smaller scale, to recapture even for a few city blocks, the smells, the tastes, the sights, the sounds and the social interactions of what life was like in the country they carry in their souls. Little Italys' cookie cutter resemblances to one another, no matter the location, are no coincidence. They are miniatures of the Italian cities the immigrants hold in their fondest memories. Today, Little Italys have become souvenirs of Italian ambience in the collective consciousness of all Canadians. They have become a template for the re-creation of such ambiance in city streets, coffee establishments, squares and mall settings throughout the country.

In every town or city where Italians have migrated, they have tried to recreate a little Italy. At first they did it out of necessity. They wanted to be near other newcomers of their same ethnic background in order to have a social network that would help them survive. Many immigrants, who were sponsored by relatives to come and live in Canada, found themselves living with or close to these people who provided them with work and housing. When they first arrived, they usually lived as boarders in the homes of relatives.

They did this usually because they didn't have any money, and the arrangement allowed them to work and to save money to buy their own homes or afford rent.

Many Italians also chose to live close to other Italian immigrants because it felt safe and familiar. In the early years of immigration to Canada, Italians were not viewed positively, and they experienced ill treatment. Little Italys were created out of a need for proximity to others they felt at home with. Italian immigrants needed to recreate an ambience of their old world in their new country, which felt unwelcoming and alien.

In Toronto, Little Italy sprang up in the early 20th century in an area called the Ward, which centred around University Avenue and College Street. It was the place where most of the early Italian immigrants settled. By the 1920s most Italians moved west of Bathurst Street, and the College-Clinton area had emerged as the city's major Little Italy. The Victorian homes that lined these streets were affordable and were bought by Italians who worked on the railways and in road construction. These homes were cheap because they were vacated by Anglo-Canadians who moved to more luxurious suburban homes. This evacuation of older residents led to the influx of Italians in the community and the opening of a large number of Italian-owned businesses along College Street. In the 1950s and the 1960s many Italians moved out of the area and headed north for the St. Clair and Dufferin Street areas, which are now called Corso Italia. By the 1960s, St. Clair had replaced College Street as the centre of Italian culture in Toronto.

Mosaic artists putting the finishing touches to their creation.

On College Street in Toronto, the Italian presence dates back to the 1890s. Italians moved up here from the Ward, and many of them settled around Mansfield Avenue and Grace Street. They opened up grocery stores that doubled as other venues. Some ventured into the banking or travel business, while others worked outside the city at various labour jobs and lived among their compatriots on the many streets around College Street.

Within the last three decades many Italians have moved out from the city to the suburbs. There are now large concentrations of Italians in Mississauga, Woodbridge, Maple, Vaughan, Richmond Hill and Downsview. Although not as large as the populations in these areas, Italians have been living and moving out to smaller Canadian areas throughout the country. Today, Little Italy's population is not only Italian but ethnically diverse. After the 1960s, the Portuguese and South American community infiltrated Little Italy in Toronto. Although many Italian families moved out to the suburbs in search of bigger homes, many businesses on St. Clair Avenue and College Street are still owned by Italians. Many of these are second-generation Italians who have bought businesses and refurbished them. Little Italy has become popular with the younger crowds because of the vibrant nightlife. Also, since the 1980s, many professionals have been buying homes in the area and renovating them.

From the late 1800s to the 1970s, thousands of Italian immigrants moved through the area. The people who remain have stories to tell that are sometimes very different from the ambiance projected by today's Little Italy. For example, Fortunato Rao arrived in Little Italy in 1952 with the largest wave of Italian immigration. Like many others, he settled around College Street, "on Brunswick Avenue, in the top floor of a house shared with a Jewish family. Rao shopped on Queen Street because College Street was more expensive." Rao shopped at Lombardi's and south on Claremont Street and was happy to find Italian products. He later moved to a residence on Clinton Street, living in an accommodation he shared with "28 men, five per room...The men cooked for themselves on a stove in the basement" but they didn't mind because their main goal was to work and to save up enough money to pay off debts incurred during immigration; others were intent on saving enough cash to buy their own homes, where they could bring their wives and families and finally settle.

Little Italys were not just ethnic enclaves, however. They were not just neighbourhoods where people lived, but they became attempts at replicating the village life the immigrants had left behind in Italy. Little Italys contained everything that an Italian city street would have, but on a smaller scale. They recreated their corner grocery stores, fish markets, fruit and produce stands, gift and garment shops, shoe stores, banks with Italian currency exchange, medical clinics where Italian was spoken, music shops, coffee shops, restaurants, dance halls and movie theatres.

In the early '60s, Italian-style bars, or *caffe'*, were described as "coffee shops" in mainstream Canadian society, but this recognition changed over time, in part as the result of deliberate marketing strategies by entrepreneurs in Little Italy. The Caffè Diplomatico (then known as the Bar Diplomatico) is one of the best-known landmarks of contemporary College Street Little Italy, a creation of its proprietors, the Mastrangelo family, including impresario and entrepreneur Rocco Mastrangelo and his brother Paul. After almost 50 years in the neighbourhood, Rocco describes with pride his role in introducing the outdoor, sidewalk patio with its signature sun umbrellas when he took over the bar in the late 1960s. "There had been other Italian bars and coffee establishments in the neighbourhood before, but with the establishment of Bar Diplomatico, in 1968, it was the added feature of the outdoor sidewalk patio, which made it an innovation soon copied by others." According to Rocco, however, the patio licence alone was not enough—it was also crucial to have an accompanying liquor licence and to encourage attractive young women to frequent the patio, often by paying them modest sums. Caffè Diplomatico in Little Italy has become a Toronto institution for coffee lovers. Affectionately known as

"The Dip" by locals, the café is often used as a set by filmmakers.

If Bar Diplomatico had become the best and most well-known coffee patio in Toronto, by the 1970s there were many other similar establishments sprouting up in various areas of College Street and St. Clair Avenue, another segment of Italian settlement where a second Little Italy began to thrive. Il Gatto Nero and Bar Italia became successful bars on College Street, while famous pasticcerias and gelaterias such as La Sem, Tre Mari and La Paloma invited Torontonians to partake in the tastes and customs of St. Clair Avenue's Little Italy. Similar to College Street, St. Clair Avenue offered Italian grocery stores, fruit and fish markets, fashion outlets, shoe stores, gift shops, book and record shops, travel agencies, churches, coffee bars, pool halls and soccer fields.

When Italians came to Canada, they could not understand the lifestyle of the people who lived here. Everyone in their separate houses, on quiet streets where everyone kept to themselves and whose only goal was walking or driving to get to work, was not their idea of life. Italians had come from a culture where city and village life was about business, yes, but also about congregating and socializing. It was about human encounter and celebration. In every city where Little Italys emerged there was a definite change in the look and feel of city space. We can see this phenomenon in every North American city where little replicas of Italian towns were recreated, and especially so on St. Clair Avenue, which was renamed Corso Italia, in Toronto.

Murray White, a reporter at the *Toronto Star*, writes in a July 2007 article: "Little Italy has changed drastically,

Tailors plying their trade.

from working-class ethnic enclave to, by the early
'90s, an eclectic mix of bars and eateries." In an interview with Edney Hendrickson, owner of the Octopus
Lounge, a hot-spot café on College Street, White writes
that the street's patrons' worry about the "ever-increasing property pressures" imposed upon them by
condo developers and city authorities. He believes
that the developers and city planners have started
what some are describing as a showdown between the
area's most recent new condo residents and the bar
and restaurant owners who were thriving on the busy
strip before their arrival. The neighbourhood may now
have to face uprooting the very area that drew people

there in the first place. Reminiscent of the 1950's "blue laws" enforcements—when Italian immigrants congregating on sidewalks for conversation were dispersed and told to go home, under the threat of potential arrest—bar and restaurant owners on College Street today are being "charged with overcrowding," having their licences suspended and forced to close down.

As the pendulum swings back from liberal ideals to conservative ones, on the fertile ground set by fear of crime and recent shootings in Toronto's entertainment districts, authorities have been dispatching police officers in Little Italys throughout the Greater Toronto Area, spurred by legislation of liquor bylaws and safety regulations. In White's interview, Hendricks expresses his frustration at the situation that is now unfolding. "They want us to have metal detectors, security guards." The condo residents would have to vote whether to keep the Octopus open or not, and because of their issue with the noise, they would surely vote it down, thus killing Octopus where it sits.

Will this and similar other events spell the end of Little Italy in Toronto? Will the condo owners and developers succeed in disintegrating the social life and ambiance of the heart of the city, like they have in so many other parts of Ontario? It remains to be seen.

Neighbourhoods come and go, and as populations change, the face of an area morphs, adjusting to the different social influences, which like the water of a river, carves its features. In a study of St. Clair Avenue for the *Journal of Historical Geography* at MacMaster University, Michael Buzzelli explains how St. Clair Avenue went from being Little Britain to Little

Italy. He documented the transformation of a Canadian cityscape to an Italian Canadian one, recounting the historical origins of St. Clair Avenue, from its roots to today. In the early part of the 20th century, people mainly of English descent lived on St. Clair. The architecture of the storefronts was Georgian, and it reflected the aesthetic sense of English culture. Much later, when English residents began moving out to the suburbs and Italian immigrants moved into the area, both houses and stores were in urgent need of renovation.

The Italians who bought the homes and businesses on St. Clair were eager to renovate them in order to give the properties a cleaner and more attractive appearance. Their renovations reflected their own cultural concepts of what was beautiful to them. Georgian features were covered up, adapted or removed in order to improve the look of the buildings, according to their own aesthetic preferences. In some places the Georgian elements of the buildings remain today, and the eclectic mix of styles is what makes St. Clair unique.

The Italian Canadian store owners who renovated St. Clair did so with the intention of giving their stores an Italian look. They introduced Toronto to outdoor gardens, archways, wrought iron balconies, balustrades, columns, cantinas, stucco, tiles and marble. Today these designs and materials are used in both domestic and commercial usage, not only in Italian Canadians' homes but everywhere throughout our cities. If St. Clair had been a street of red brick Georgian shops and homes, with wood trim, the Italians changed all that to include the more modern look of light-coloured stucco. They also replaced wooden and vinyl floors and countertops with marble and granite, a trend that has spread like wild fire in the building and renovation styles of today, both at the commercial and the residential level.

One interesting change that has affected the Canadian lifestyle and had its origins in Toronto's Little Italy is the window and door space of coffee shops and restaurants. Before Italians came to Toronto, restaurants and cafés had a solid, wooden door that led into a vestibule and then into a side public space. If there was a front window, it was usually opaque so that the people dining inside could not see the people walking by outside, and vice versa. Italians who bought these businesses made a few adaptations that changed public space and the way people relate when going out to eat and socialize. They removed the wooden doors and replaced them with glass doors positioned in the centre of the storefront's plate-glass window. The interior walls of the vestibules were knocked down, opening up the eating space. They also added outdoor eating areas, which, though popular today, had never been seen in Canada. These changes allowed people to eat outside at sidewalk cafés during the summer months. It is the element that has changed Canadian cities for the better, giving them that *je ne sais quoi* appeal that was reserved only for European cities. What was once only found in Little Italy has now become a common trend everywhere in Canada.

Ottawa has one of the oldest Little Italys. Situated in Centretown West, it is the cultural centre of Ottawa's Italian community. With Albert Street to the north, Carling Avenue to the south, the O-train tracks to the west and Bell Street to the east, Ottawa's Little Italy intersects with Chinatown. It was initially settled around 1900 by Italian immigrants. After a fire at a small Murray Street Chapel, the Church of Saint Anthony of Padua was built in its place in 1913. The new church helped cement the early immigrants' connection with the neighbourhood.

After World War II, a new wave of Italian immigrants was joined by other European immigrants, such as the Ukrainians and the Polish. In more recent years, immigrants from China and Vietnam have made it their neighbourhood. Although many Italian people do not live in the area, the title of "Little Italy" has stuck. It is home to many Italian businesses and stores. The Italian Week Festival, one of the biggest celebrations of Italian culture in Ottawa, is held on Preston Street every June, since 1974. Preston Street is marked at Carling Avenue by a metal arch lit in the colours of the Italian flag.

Montréal's Little Italy ("Petite Italie") runs along Saint Lawrence Boulevard, between Saint-Zotique and Jean Talon streets. It is one of the main centres of Montréal's Italian community and has many Italian shops and restaurants, along with the Jean Talon market and the famous Church of the Madonna Della Difesa. This church was built by Italian immigrants to commemorate the apparition of the Virgin Mary in La Difesa area of Campobasso, in the Italian region of Molise. Montréal's Little Italy, just like Toronto's, was the site of much celebration when Italy won the 2006 FIFA World Cup of soccer. This little replica of an Italian city neighbourhood is located in the Montréal district of Rosemont-La Petite Patrie.

Little Italy in Vancouver is located in the eastern part of the city, in the Grandview Woodland neighbourhood. The area was historically an ethnic enclave of Italians. In the beginning, businesses and cultural facilities of this Little Italy were located along Commercial Drive, which is still a social centre in eastern Vancouver. Between 1930 and 1970, Italians were influential in this part of the city. After World War I, Italians settled in the Commercial Drive district, which was one of the most impoverished areas of Vancouver, and Italian immigrants revitalized the neighbourhood. A combination of cultural assimilation, other foreign immigration and Italian movement to the suburbs led to a decline in the concentration and influence of Italians in Vancouver by 1975.

Today there are many Italian businesses, cultural groups and Italians living in the Greater Vancouver area, but no one area is predominant as a Little Italy. The only area that has a significant Italian presence is Burnaby Heights. East Hastings Street, between Boundary and Duthie, is another area where the Italian community has many cafés, restaurants, delis and clothing stores with imported goods from Italy. These areas also have two Catholic churches that offer Italian masses: St. Helen's and Holy Cross. Many older Italian men get together at Confederation Park in Vancouver, where they play the game of bocce.

There is also a Little Italy in Winnipeg. Here the Italian neighbourhood is located on Corydon Avenue, between Stafford Street and Pembina Highway. The area contains many Italian boutiques and some of the city's best restaurants.

In many cities, however, Little Italys have lost the presence of ethnic Italians to the new waves of immigrants from other communities, such as the Portuguese, Jamaican, Chinese and South American. Regardless, the stores and businesses have kept an

Italian flavour and atmosphere. Italian cafés, restaurants and social clubs still thrive. The people who come to shop in these Italian businesses are not only Italians, but people of every ethnicity who come to get a taste of Italian food, fashion, but most of all Italian lifestyle.

Little Italys started out as areas where Italians lived and did business. Today, they have become the trendy places where Canadians go to find fine restaurants, great fashion and an Italian ambiance without having to travel to Italy. As Italian Canadians moved out into the suburbs, they brought with them the same wish to recreate community spaces such as cafés, pastry shops and bakeries where they could enjoy Italian delicacies. One can see the popularity of Italian-style ambiances replete with Italian terracotta flowerpots, paintings of archways and, of course, Italian music playing in the background. And espresso bars are everywhere.

If Italian Canadians are assimilating into the existing culture, then the face of Anglo-Canada has been changed also by the Italian presence. No longer places of just beer pubs and fast-food joints, Canadian cities offer everything Italian, with style and panache as their higher end fare of social and cultural life.

CHAPTER ELEVEN

NATIONAL UNITY: HOW ITALIANS HELPED KEEP CANADA TOGETHER

There is no such thing as a model or ideal Canadian. What could be more absurd than the concept of an "all Canadian boy or girl"? A society which emphasizes uniformity is one which creates intolerance and hate.

–Pierre Trudeau

C anada is a country of multiculturalism. It is metaphorically described as a mosaic. Within its borders it is home to people of every ethnic and religious background, originating from countries all over the world. But it was not long ago that Canada was a much different place.

Since its inception as a nation, and until Pierre Trudeau's new era of multiculturalism, Canada was a country of what has been aptly named "Two Solitudes," Although stretching from the Atlantic to the Pacific coasts, Canada's two major players were

Ontario and Québec. Right from the beginning, Upper and Lower Canada were the stage for the social and political debates that created our nation. From those early times, the coming together and separation of the two cultural groups that inhabited these areas were the catalysts for what we now call Canada.

Québec and Ontario have always been the two provinces that dictated the outcome of our future. When the French colonized the shores of the St. Lawrence, they staked out their territory on Canadian soil. So, too, did the English when they won the battle on the Plains of Abraham and established their sovereignty over Canadian territory. Since that brief, but decisive battle, decades of tension and political conflict followed. It wasn't until Confederation in 1867 that French Québec alongside the rest of English-speaking Canada came to terms with its unique linguistic and social differences. With Confederation came the official acceptance by the government as to the viability of both groups as the founding cultures of our country. The importance of keeping both languages and cultures was officially affirmed. A bilingual country was thus established, where Canadians would speak English and/or French. Québec became free to maintain its French language and culture within Canada's larger English culture.

Confederation granted the francophone majority in Québec some degree of political autonomy, especially in the areas of education, culture and local issues. Québec became known for its separateness of language and social institutions: schools, churches, hospitals and other social and political offices. It wasn't until the beginning of the 20th century, when other ethnic groups started coming into the country, that things began to change.

In the early 1900s, the new immigrants coming into Québec were mainly Jews and Italians. They built synagogues and Italian Catholic churches, which provided social and community services. Within the separateness of French and English ethnic communities, these new immigrants formed their own separate ethnic clusters. Within the Italian communities, family and neighbourhood relations were strong. They stuck together in close-knit associations. They operated boarding houses for other Italian immigrant workers. Many of them opened stores in Montréal's inner city neighbourhoods. Their children studied French in Montréal's Catholic school system. This was mostly because the Italians had more in common culturally with the French. Both groups were Catholic and many intermarried. It wasn't until after World War II that Italians started sending their children to English schools.

In *Immigrant Culture: The Identity of the Voiceless People,* author Marco Micone writes about his experience growing up in Montréal. He explains that the "Duplessis regime of Québec was so grovelling and blind toward the reality of Anglophone power that Québec's English-speaking educational authorities could quite freely plot and put into effect the ultimate stratagem for increasing the number of English-speaking people in Québec and making French Canadians a smaller minority in Canada as a whole." In order to achieve this, "they attracted a majority of young people whose native language was neither French nor English." According to Micone, marginalized immigrant children, who had learned English instead of French, once they graduated, found themselves in the precarious situation of not being hired in the professions they had aspired to. It was what Micone believes the Québecers wanted all along, which was to keep the Italians, and all immigrants in general, "in a marginal position and remain there for a long time." This would keep them out of the elite professions and "civil service careers that the francophones have been so successful in protecting for themselves."

Language was more than an issue of culture; it was a marker of social inclusion or marginality. If learning French gave Italian immigrants a ticket of acceptance within the Québec culture, learning English, which they believed to be the language of power in a mainly English Canada, rendered them even more powerless.

Many of the immigrants who arrived in Canada after the war did so to improve their standard of living. They came to what they believed to be an English-speaking North America, and therefore they wanted their children to learn English. English was viewed as the language of success, and it was the reason that Italian immigrants chose to send their children to English-language Catholic schools. By 1961, 70 percent of Italian children were attending schools in the English-Catholic system. However, even though they chose English as their language, Italians were not assimilated into the English community of Québec. They kept most contact with the French community. Most of all they remained secluded within their own Italian ethnic communities, and as a result they maintained their own Italian Canadian cultural identity, more so perhaps than Italians in other Canadian cities.

In 1950 many Italians arrived in Canada.

In the 1960s, Québec nationalism was on the rise. After a century of Confederation, French Canadians felt as if they were still second-class citizens, not just in Canada but also within the borders of their own province. English-speaking residents of Québec made more money than their French-speaking counter-parts, according to bilingualism polls of the times. The Parti Québecois and the Rassemblement Pour l'Independence Nationale came together to transform the inequalities and imbalances of power that existed between the French and the English. The question of language became important. With a decreased birth rate in the French-speaking population and an increase in English-speaking people living in Québec, it became urgent to maintain the French language or risk cultural assimilation. Everyone living in Québec, including the immigrant population, was encouraged to speak French. Learning French was especially imposed on new immigrant groups. Anglo-Québecers were protected by acquired educational rights from having to learn French. Many immigrant groups, however, including the Italians, believed this policy was unfair.

In *The Italians of Québec: Key Participants in Contemporary Linguistic and Political Debates,* Paul-Andre' Linteau writes: "in 1968, in the small Montréal suburb of Saint-Leonard, the language question sparked violent incidents between Italians and French Canadians. The issue was the following: should the municipality's Italian immigrants be forced to send their children to French schools or should they be left free to choose their language of instruction? The conflict stirred passionate debate, turbulent meetings and street battles between members of the two groups." This particular debate was indicative of a pervasive problem throughout the province of Québec in the '60s and '70s.

As the third-largest group in Québec after the French and the English, the Italians were caught in the middle of the language debate. The majority of them reacted negatively to language laws that were instituted between 1968 and 1977, which demanded that all Québec residents learn French. The language laws were seen as restrictive by many Italian immigrants. Being limited to French was not viewed as the road to success within the larger context of North America. Some Italian groups opposed the French language laws by supporting English-language presses and the English school system. They were led by the *Consiglio Educativo Italo-Canadese* of Québec. Other

Italian groups tried to convince the political parties to negotiate the use of English along with French. They mostly relied on the help of the Liberal Party and were in favour of a bilingual Québec. This stand made them supporters of the federal Liberal antinationalist position of Pierre Elliot Trudeau and opponents of nationalist Liberals and advocates of independence.

The majority of Italians wanted free choice. To them this meant having the right to educate their children in English, if they so chose. They believed that English was the language needed for social and economic advancement and that English was necessary to ensure that their children could move out of Québec if they wished to, and so they encouraged their children to learn English. Without realizing it, the Italians in Québec found themselves as major players in their province's language debate. They were at the core of the ethnic and culturally diverse groups of Québec that influenced that province's future.

Today, the Ministry of Cultural Communities deals with promoting third-language teaching of heritage languages, Italian being one of them. The language debate that spanned the '60s and continues today gave the Italians a strong political awareness. Because they had to choose sides, they were forced to look at themselves, their identity and their goals as a people. Many people took on leadership roles to try to resolve these issues. Many Italian political organizations sprung up, the main one being *Le Congres Nationale des Italo-Canadiens de Québec*. In essence, because of the language debate between English and French, the Italian community of Québec grew stronger, creating a close-knit community life. Within these family and community organizations, they found their own unique voice. Many of them still speak Italian as well as English and/or French. More Italians in Québec speak Italian than Italians living in other Canadian provinces today. They took on strong political views and played an active role in the language debate. How did this debate affect Canada as a whole?

Italians were the third party, so to speak. Between the two discordant sides they brought a third point of view, a new language and a new ethnicity. Their arrival brought a sort of common denominator for both cultures. Filippo Salvatore, professor at Ryerson University in Toronto, explains: "If this country is still in one piece, it is also thanks to Italian Canadians. In the last referendum we were decisive: our votes prevented the secession of Québec." This, he says, "despite the fact that more similarities exist between the Québecois and us than between the Anglophones and us. We have always helped this country search for its identity, though; we do so by looking for our own. Participating in such important processes means being protagonists."

Salvatore also says that when people ask him where he was born he says "Québec." He believes that Québec was here first, and then came the rest of Canada. This country, according to Salvatore, has historically been a country of two cultural and linguistic solitudes.

The Italians were the first group to make both sides take a good look at each other. If Québec didn't separate from the rest of Canada, it was because of the immigrant vote, which at the time was when separation was most likely to happen. In essence, the Italian presence was the child that kept Canada's marriage together—the cultural glue that kept the country from cracking apart. They were here before multicultural-ism was ever even a thought, never mind an institu-tion. They were one of the first important pieces of what was to become the country's great cultural mosaic.

CHAPTER TWELVE

PIERRE TRUDEAU AND MULTICULTURALISM: TIES TO ITALIANS IN CANADA

For the past 150 years nationalism has been a retro-grade idea. By an historic accident Canada has found itself approximately seventy-five years ahead of the rest of the world in the formation of a multinational state, and I happen to believe that the hope of mankind lies in multinationalism.

–Pierre Trudeau

If Canada is a multicultural utopia today, we owe it all to Pierre Trudeau. It was his timely vision of a country that would allow every ethnic group to maintain its cultural identity within the rights and responsibilities of Canadian citizenship that made Canada a mosaic rather than a melting pot. Under his inspiration, diversity became a positive value in Canada. With his charismatic leadership, Trudeau as a Liberal prime minister successfully shifted the mindset of an entire nation. Because of changing demographics as a result of a large influx of immigrants, Canada was no longer a country of only English and French but was becoming a multicultural, multilingual society. Belonging to a different ethnicity and having a separate identity and culture was no longer a shameful thing, as it had been until that time, but something to be proud of. Under Trudeau's leadership, heritage became something to be treasured. He taught Canadians that only through honouring our own separate histories can we truly begin to love and cherish our new country. His was the paradigm that espouses the belief that only out of self-respect can individuals begin to love the world. His was a vision of cultural pluralism.

Trudeau made the Canadian mosaic our cultural cliché and our main national characteristic. "There is no official culture, nor does any ethnic group take precedence over any other. No citizen or group of citizens is any other than Canadian, and all should be treated fairly." He believed that if the Canadian state respected people for who they were, they in turn would be grateful and loyal to that state.

Pierre Trudeau played a major role in allowing minority groups to gain access to Canada's ruling circles. Because of new multicultural laws passed in the '60s and '70s, today all Canadians have equal access to education, employment and discourse in politics. It may be surprising to new Canadians entering the country today to know that human rights were not always part of the constitution before Trudeau.

For all the immigrants living in Canada in the '60s, these laws made a monumental difference. Italian people were both influential in these changes and influenced by them. Their struggles led their associations to persuade political leaders to respond to their wide range of problems and needs. The dialogue that ensued from the Italians' efforts was one of the main catalysts for the Liberal government's response to such issues. The policies of multiculturalism were in essence a response to the needs of a new multiethnic Canadian population, of which the Italian community was one of its largest components. Other ethnic groups involved in multi-ethnic Canada were the Germans, the Jewish, the Polish and the Ukrainians. How did the Italians contribute to the Liberal government's fostering of the multicultural ideals?

It is important to remember that Canada, under the Conservative government's rule in the '50s and early '60s, had a totally different political landscape. According to Julian Fantino, former chief of the Toronto Police, "blue laws" were still in place. Ontario, and especially Toronto, was a very puritanical place in those days. Sundays were considered days consisting of family and prayer. Public bars were closed, and people were not allowed to congregate on sidewalks or city corners. They were imagined to be up to no good and dangerous, as if their getting together would surely result in a riot or other criminal activity.

Italian immigrants in the '50s and '60s spent their evenings and Sundays in the small Italian bars on College Street and St. Clair Avenue in Toronto. They wanted to socialize and to listen to Italian soccer games on the radio, which in those days were not televised. Sometimes they would continue their enthusiastic talks about the games on the sidewalks outside their coffee shops, just like they had done in Italy. This innocent pastime was viewed suspiciously by the police who would come around to disperse them, frightened by the loud, passionate discussions of these sports fans. It was really a sad misunderstanding brought on by a clash of cultures. English authorities feared congregation and loud conversation, while Italian immigrants loved social gatherings and the enjoyment of talking with friends and family about their favourite sport.

But it wasn't just the social environment that alienated new immigrants. Although Canada was a country of conservative rules and regulations, it did not provide such rules and regulated safety measures for Italians and other ethnic workers. The immigrants who had been arriving since the '50s worked mostly in construction jobs. Safety on work sites was not regulated, and many workers were seriously injured or lost their lives. In addition, job advancement, even at the construction level, was impossible for them. Management jobs always went to the more established Canadians with English names. Many of these immigrant men couldn't go to school because they were working to support their families and couldn't speak English very well. Their children didn't have much hope of faring any better, either. In those days, entry to university was determined by passing a specific IQ test. Students who didn't meet its requirements were denied access to post-secondary education. Of course, as was learned later, these IQ tests were found to be biased against immigrant children, who had not been exposed to certain cultural factors present in the tests. This factor, combined with teachers' and administrators' view of Italians as mere labourers, streamed many Italian young people toward trades and vocational schools. It would take decades before things began to change.

Attacking the rock with pick and shovel to forge a path for the railway (1918).

Italian immigrants have been known for being law-abiding citizens who didn't cause waves politically in Canada. The unfairness of education procedures that affected their children, as well as the many unfair practices in the world of labour, propelled the Italian community to seek change. Particularly in the construction industry, these immigrant workers were exploited almost as slaves. There was a disregard for hiring laws, safety of the workers on the job sites, lack of pensions or insurance for injured workers and firing of workers if they failed to abide by their company's demands. The people who worked these jobs were largely Italian. They were also not protected by any laws or unions. Eventually, the situation got so bad, especially with the incident of the Italian workers killed in Hogg's Hollow in Toronto, that immigrant workers united themselves to take action. They went on strike and demanded better work conditions. They formed groups that lobbied for safety regulations and better treatment. They found their way to the NDP party leaders, who were listening and trying to help with the social issues of these immigrants.

Elio Costa, a professor of Italian Literature at York University and holder of the Mariano Elia Chair in Italian Studies, explains: "The situation really bordered on the unbearable, therefore all parties tackled the problem and looked for one permanent solution. The Liberals found one, due to their ideological specificity that allowed them to understand emergencies and respond in a timely fashion. In those years, the Liberal Party also had an additional bonus: the Federal leader was Pierre Trudeau, the keenest politician in modern Canada. Now you see how the problem of equality between immigrants and Canadians became paramount."

So, multiculturalism was born to assuage the need of these new Canadians. It was a much-needed solution to address these immigrants' problems of fixing labour laws, education and equality of rights. Multiculturalism then was more than an ideological concept. It became an umbrella solution for the many real, social problems faced by new immigrants, who at the time were mostly Italian.

Pierre Trudeau was the official father of a multicultural Canadian society. He grasped the concept at the right time and iconized it in our national identity, though he did not come to it in a vacuum. Emergencies and injustices were so evident in the dealings with immigrants during the '50s and '60s that reform policies had to be put in place to correct the problems. These reforms took the commitment of many people, from community leaders of the ethnic groups in question, to journalists and other media representatives.

Dan Iannuzzi, publisher of *Corriere Canadese,* and Johnny Lombardi, founder of multicultural radio station CHIN, comes to mind. Iannuzzi dedicated his entire career to multiculturalism in Canada, and he did this before multiculturalism ever became a national concept. He worked tirelessly in international and multicultural media. A third-generation Italian Canadian, in 1954 he founded the newspaper *Corriere Canadese,* in Italian, to serve the Italian community in Canada. He was one of the first people to give Italian Canadians a voice. He kept them informed on issues pertaining to them, happening in both Canada and Italy. As technology grew, Iannuzzi kept up with the times. Although continuing with his leadership in *Corriere Canadese,* he also became executive producer of the multilingual programming on City TV in Toronto in 1979. Also, as the Italian community began to change, he offered second- and third-generation Italians a new English version of *Corriere Canadese,* which goes under the publication name of *Tandem* today. This newspaper addresses issues of the Italian community, but it caters more to the needs of newer generations.

One cannot talk about multiculturalism in Canada without also thinking of Johnny Lombardi. He was the face that personified multiculturalism for Italians living in Canada. In his benevolent, fatherly way, he made it palatable for Italians to love Toronto. His beloved CHIN radio station reached millions of Italians throughout the country, giving them a voice and a unity previously unparalleled. He greeted thousands of Italians in Canadian towns in their own language, with words of hope and praise for their often discounted and unspoken efforts. His famous introductory words, which have been recorded and are often still used on CHIN morning radio shows, were "Buon giorno cari..." (Good morning dear ones...) and will not be forgotten by the thousands of listeners of his morning talk show. He urged his listeners to work hard and to love each other, which were his philosophies for success and a happy life. The words "Fa' na bona jobba" (Do a good job) and "Voletevi bene, assai, assai, assai!" (Love each other, very much, very much, very much!) are inscribed on the walls of his radio station and also in the minds and hearts of Italian Canadians everywhere.

Lombardi dedicated himself to the cause of multiculturalism and to the celebration of cultural diversity. "He was light years ahead of many with his early commitment to this cause. He always felt that Toronto and its wonderful ethnic mosaic had something special to share with and guide the rest of the world. Former Prime Minister Pierre Trudeau was a good friend of Johnny, also a proud Liberal, and they had many discussions about multiculturalism," said his son, Lenny. According to Lenny, Johnny Lombardi "had a significant influence on the former prime minister."

Trudeau, influenced by Johnny's multilingual ideology, once stated, "Canada is not a bilingual country, we are a multilingual country." Indeed, this was Johnny's dream, to propagate a message of tolerance and understanding. Johnny Lombardi's famous CHIN was Ontario's first multicultural and multilingual radio station. CHIN is now broadcast in more than

30 languages, with its music and message reaching a wide range of cultural communities. The radio station started out serving the Toronto area with CHIN AM 1540 and FM 100.7. It then spread to the Ottawa and Gatineau region on 97.9 FM CJLL. Today CHIN programs are available via satellite across North America on Anik F1, Ku-Band, Transponder 18, and listeners worldwide can also tune in on the Internet at www.chinradio.com.

Johnny Lombardi's radio station gave Italians first in Toronto and then throughout Canada a unified identity. It also gave thousands of other ethnicities an opportunity to be heard within Canada's mosaic. Based on his own experience of poverty and dealing with prejudice, Lombardi brought passion and con- viction to his fight for open-mindedness and common respect. It was through music and open communica- tion that he was able to bridge many gaps between the cultures with the common thread of radio. Music was his love, and he believed it to be the universal lan- guage that could unite all people.

Giovanni Barbalinardo, or Johnny Lombardi, as he was later known, was born in 1915 in the humble area of the Ward where his family lived before World War I. His parents Leonardo and Teresa Barbalinardo were from the town of Pisticci, in the Italian region of Basilicata. Amidst poverty and difficult living condi- tions, the family moved from rooming house to room- ing house within the Ward, in search of a better deal. As their situation improved, they eventually moved to College Street, near Clinton, a better area of Toronto that had an emerging Italian community.

Johnny Lombardi grew up on College Street's Little Italy, and it was on that street that he lived and made a successful life for himself, one that would have such a positive effect on so many Canadians. As a child, Johnny studied music, teaching himself to play the harmonica, the bugle and the trumpet, and winning several gold medals. When he was nine he shined shoes at a mobile shoeshine stand near the Shea Theatre in downtown Toronto, which is no longer there. When he wasn't shining shoes, he was at the theatre trying to catch a glimpse of the performances, and to his delight, one day he was given a chance to participate. He decided to study music through the charitable graces of the Boys' K Club and the Columbus Boys Club, which were service clubs for underprivileged kids. Out of his love for music and performance, he pursued a career as a trumpet player and band leader. With the advent of World War II, he served in the Canadian Armed Forces, and when he returned from overseas, he became the owner of a grocery store business at the corner of Manning Street and Dundas in Toronto. It was in this store that he met Lena Crisologo one day when she came in shopping with her mother. Taken by her beauty, Johnny married Lena in 1949. Their marriage of 52 years was blessed with three children and five grandchildren.

Johnny Lombardi's grocery business thrived in the '50s, and he soon relocated to 637 College, near Grace Street. While Lena and his sister Carmie ran the supermarket, Johnny kept busy with other interests, such as organizing concerts, radio programmes, record importing, as well as food and specialty importing. He brought in singers from Italy for concerts at Massey Hall, Maple Leaf Gardens, the O'Keefe Centre (now the Hummingbird Centre), Roy Thompson Hall and even Eaton's College and Bay store theatre hall.

He produced Italian radio programs on CHUM and CKFH radio to promote his supermarket, his concerts and community events, such as park shows. He also started the record label Bravo Records & Music, to promote Italian Canadian singers.

In the early '60s, Johnny turned his never-ending energy and attention to the new immigrants coming to Toronto from Europe. With the growing need for more radio time, he applied for a multicultural radio station, and CHIN Radio launched, opening its studios and offices above Johnny Lombardi's supermarket in 1966. With this eventful multilingual radio launch, Canadian multicultural history was in the making.

Johnny's perceptiveness in capturing the essence of his era was what made him an icon in Canada's multiculturalism history. With passion and humility, he served the community in which he was born and lived his whole life. He will always be remembered for his multi-ethnic broadcasting for over 50 years; his very own International Picnic—the world's largest free picnic —which celebrated its 40th anniversary, along with CHIN radio, in 2006. Today, his radio station continues its multicultural programming, in addition to his Sunday television programme *Festival Italiano di Johnny Lombardi,* broadcast live from the CHIN building.

With his passing at the age of 86, Canadians, especially Italian Canadians, lost a friend and a hero. His fame in multicultural radio and television programming was augmented by his benevolent nature and giving spirit. He was an active fundraiser for many Canadian charities, of which the Hospital for Sick Children was his favourite. He hosted many telethons and radiothons over his career and sat on the boards of several charitable organizations. Among his many awards, he received the Order of Ontario and the Order of Canada, as well as the Ted Rogers Graham Award from the Canadian Association of Radio Broadcasters. He was a pioneer in his field, and he will always be remembered as the father of multicultural media and broadcasting in Canada.

Canada's multicultural policies, however, were the result of many factors. The mid-1960s were marked by increasing troubled English-French relations in Canada. The government appointed a Royal Commission to study the problem and recommend solutions. The Royal Commission on Bilingualism and Biculturalism held hearings across Canada. In 1969 the Bilingual and Bicultural Act became a law. Immigrants all over the country made it clear to the commissioners that they were unhappy with being left out of the discourse of their country. Being neither English nor French, they still felt Canadian, but because they didn't belong to the first two groups, they felt left out.

Many of these immigrants were Italians, but there were many other groups, such as the Ukrainians and the Germans, who also wanted representation. They urged a new model of citizen participation within the context of the larger society. They wanted a system that would address all the ethnic groups living in Canada, based on public acceptance of differences and support of cultural pluralism. Rather than the melting pot of the United States, they preferred the idea of a mosaic, where all the unique parts form one whole. It was argued that ethnicity did not determine Canada's identity, but rather the identity of the people did. The Royal Commission agreed and brought their findings to the government, and the first multicultural policy was announced in 1971. French and English were declared Canada's official languages, but ethnic diversity was declared to be a positive feature of Canadian society, worthy of preservation and development. Multiculturalism became a law in 1982. Later in 1988, Bill C-93 was passed as the Multicultural Act.

The Italian immigrants faced many struggles in the workplace and in schools during the '50s and '60s in Canada. They faced difficulties with working conditions in the areas of regulation and safety, along with discrimination based on their ethnicity. Politically, they became a big voting chunk of the population. At first aided by the NDP with labour issues, their issues served to become an attractive platform for the success of the Liberals. The Liberal party, led by Pierre Trudeau, responded to the concerns of Italian immigrants by promising them change and improvement to their situation. After becoming acquainted with their issues and those of other new immigrants, the Liberal party implemented multiculturalism. The problems immigrants faced were unmet by previous governments and were in dire need of being addressed. It was because of the Italians that the Liberal party of Canada rose to the occasion. The country of tolerance and open dialogue we have today between the different ethnic groups is as a result of the first immigrants, who had to fight for basic human rights as students, workers and citizens of Canada.

Today, we have a Canada where every person is equal and has rights and privileges. The multicultural policy ensures that Canadian citizens can participate as members of society regardless of racial, ethnic, cultural or religious background. Multiculturalism promotes gaining an understanding of people from all cultures, despite language, religious beliefs, political and social views, or national origins. It does not require people to shed their own beliefs and values in order to accept one another. Instead, multiculturalism acknowledges that there are many ways in which the world can be viewed and lived in. Multiculturalism essentially promotes respect for people's distant cultural identity, while ensuring that common Canadian values are upheld.

CHAPTER THIRTEEN

FAMOUS ITALIAN CANADIANS

Italian Canadians have demonstrated an extraordinary ability to integrate, associate and organize...Today, they are part of every segment of society, and their contribution is widely acknowledged.
–Michaëlle Jean, Governor General of Canada

I talians have been a part of Canadian culture since its very beginnings. They have participated in the history of this country from their role as explorers, then builders, and finally, as common participants in every facet of Canadian life. In the book *Made in Canada: The Italian Way*, the mayor of Toronto, David Miller writes, "If anyone wonders why Toronto has its motto, 'Diversity is Our Strength,' they need look no further than the city's Italian community. For some people, the phrase 'Toronto's Italian community' merely evokes thoughts of the bars and restaurants along College St. West or the shops and cafés near St. Clair West and Dufferin. But of course, the accomplishments of Toronto's Italian population have helped to shape every aspect of life in every part of the city."

The story of the Italians in Canada is filled with sweat, toil and sacrifice. As one of the first ethnic groups to break the gap of a bicultural country, they had to push hard against walls of opposition and conservative mind-sets. Their determination and strong family and community cohesion helped them to mobilize their strength toward the goals of fairness and common understanding. With obedience and respect to civic duty and government laws, these immigrants organized themselves and elected leaders to represent their cause, within the framework of fair democratic politics. Through their efforts, many of them and their children gained financial success. As in most immigrant stories, their dreams for their children's futures did, for the most part, actualize. Their children would indeed have a better future than they did.

"The presence and influence of Italians in Canada in the twentieth century was most strongly imprinted on the landscape of the country by men who built. Still, our world is not made of buildings and sidewalks alone," says Kenneth Bagnell in *Canadese: A Portrait of the Italian Canadians.* But, as he continues to explain in his book, "by the 1960s, names with an Italian cadence were sounding in the ears of Canadians like a familiar tune, and influencing national taste in decisive ways." These were not the names of Italians known only within the enclaves of the Italian community, but names that resounded within the larger Canadian community. Names of developers such as Tridel, Del Zotto, Fram, Metrus, Con-Drain,

Con-Elco, Falvo Steel, Bot, Pemberton Group, Camrost and Marel are indicative of the influence Italians had on the growth of Ontario cities alone. University branches and libraries are being named after some of the people who were most influential.

Upon entering the University of Toronto, Erindale Campus' new library, for my research for this book, I was surprised to see the name inscribed on the interior wall, which read *The Muzzo Library*. Curious about the name, I approached the girl at the front desk, who didn't know the origin of the library's name, either, but she Googled it nevertheless and printed the information for me. What I discovered was the name of Marco Muzzo, one of the most influential builders in the Greater Toronto Area.

When Muzzo died of cancer on December 5, 2005, at the age of 72, "the bells rang," wrote John Barber in the *Globe and Mail*. They were not the bells "of the picturesque village churches of his native Friuli, the region of northeastern Italy that has produced a disproportionate share of modern Toronto's master builders, but ring-tones chiming from one end to the other of the 100-mile city on the north shore of Lake Ontario that he did so much to build. The message was 'The King is Dead,' said one among the huge network of colleagues. Mr. Muzzo cultivated his 55-year career in construction and development. 'He was the No. 1 guy.'"

Marco Muzzo emerged as a top developer not only for his attention to detail and quality but also for treating people fairly. His motto was "What's good for buyers is good for builders." He believed in focusing on the needs of homebuyers and in providing them with quality, affordable accommodation. "We cannot allow government policy at any level to burden new homebuyers with ever-increasing taxes, levies, fees, higher land costs, new design and code requirements, or chronic approval delays," he said. "These burdens will erode our ability to offer value to our customers, which will ultimately drive them to the resale market or out of the market altogether."

Muzzo developed much of Woodbridge, where he lived. Mississauga mayor Hazel McCallion explained that the Erin Mills Community is also one of Marco Muzzo's many developments. She says: "people are very happy and we get few complaints because he did it well. He built very acceptable communities that responded to the needs of people and he demonstrated a concern for people."

In downtown Toronto, Muzzo purchased St. Michael College from the University of Toronto. The university needed money to keep its doors open, so they decided to sell the land at St. Mary and Bay Street, but it was worried about losing its green space. Muzzo didn't let them down. He built around the green space, ensuring its preservation, on top of which, he made a donation of $5 million to the school. In recognition of his kindness, the university conferred him with an honorary doctorate degree and named some of its buildings after him. If he was respected by the community, it was not only because of his achievements in the building and sales of residential communities but also because of his great contributions to charitable organizations, including Sick Children's Hospital, Women's College Hospital, Sunnybrook Hospital, Princess Margaret Hospital and many other institutions.

Julie Di Lorenzo, past president of the Greater Toronto Home Builders Association (GTHBA), led the

Primo I. Di Luca, past president of the Famee Furlane, receiving the Order of Canada (1980).

annual Hall of Fame Member of the Year and Presidential Award of Merit Announcements. Announcing the Hall of Fame induction recipient, Di Lorenzo described the late Marco Muzzo as "one of the most visionary entrepreneurs the province of Ontario has ever seen. He coached people with promise and built an empire around those great people."

The names of Italians who contributed to Canadian business and achieved professional success are listed in the Canadian-Italian Business and Professional Association (CIBPA) of Canada. The CIBPA was founded in 1949 in Montréal and was created as a non-profit organization to promote and unite business people and professionals of Italian origin. The National Federation of CIBPA was established in 1987, and today it is comprised of 12 chapters across Canada. Through its lists of members we find Marco Muzzo, and his son Steven Muzzo, president and CEO of Ozz Corporation, a business that fosters planet friendly electricity consumption.

Some well-known Canadian companies whose founders or company leaders are Italian Canadians and are included in the CIBPA list may ring a bell to most readers, and they include:

Inniskillin Wines (Donald Ziraldo)
Italpasta (Joe Vitale)
RBC Canada (Senior Executive Vice-President Elisabetta Recchi-Bigsby)
Alba Tours/Skyservice (Gianni Bragagnolo)
The Hummingbird Centre (Daniel Brambilla)
The Remington Group; Bratty and Partners (Rudolph Bratty)
Capri Films Distributions (Tony Cianciotta)
Manulife Financial (Dominic D'Alessandro)
Metrus Group, Con-Drain, Con-Elco (Fred De Gasperis)
Liberty Entertainment Group (Nick Di Donato)
Cineplex Odeon (Sam Di Michele)
Cabot Trust (Consiglio Di Nino)
Falvo Steel (Franco Falvo)
St. Joseph Printing Corporation (Gaetano Gagliano)
Corriere Canadese/Tandem (Dan Iannuzzi)
Vin Bon & Cilento Wines (Angelo Locilento)
Lovat Inc. (Richard Lovat)
Shade-o-Matic (Norberto Marocco)
Capri Films Production (Gabriella Martinelli)
Numage Trading (Gesualdo Mastruzzo)
Equinox Films (Michael Mosca)
Diamante Architectural Firm (Paolo Palamara)
Colombo Importing Ltd – Jan K. Overweel Ltd. (Arturo Pelliccione)
Canada Trust (Gina Scola)
Azure magazine (Sergio Sgaramella)
Zanchin Group Number 7 Honda (Giuseppe Zanchin)
MacDonald's Canada (Louie Mele)
Faema (Mike Di Donato)

Countless others exist, of whom I am not aware of and to whom I apologize for not being able to mention.

The names of Italian Canadian food and beverage companies such as Primo, Brio, Mastro, Tre Stelle and Milano, Catelli and Italpasta became common logos not only in magazine and television commercials but also more frequently on the sides of transport trucks along our national highways, bringing their merchandise from city centres to supermarkets throughout Canada. The same goes for fruit markets that later became large supermarkets, such as Longo's, Badali's, Cataldi's, Bruno's, Fortino's and countless others. At first these businesses catered to the Italian immigrant community but were then discovered by everyone and are now renowned for their top quality, gourmet fare.

The story is much the same for many other names of people and products that have infiltrated our common, contemporary, Canadian consciousness. "Faema," the famous espresso maker company, was first imported to Toronto by Mike Di Donato, and it soon made its way into the espresso bars of Little Italys throughout North America and in the homes of many Italian Canadians. With the growing popularity of espresso bars in our culture, Faema has become a common name that signifies a good quality cup of espresso or cappuccino.

On the Telelatino television program *Persona*, Mike Di Donato explained how when he first came to Toronto in the 1950s, he was looking for a place where he could get a good cup of espresso coffee, but he couldn't find one. It was this simple wish that gave him the idea to begin importing coffee machines to

Toronto. He saw a need for something that was such a basic staple for Italian Canadians. He believed that there was a market for his coffeemakers and he had much success with their sales in the '60s and '70s. The unprecedented popularity of espresso bars and skyrocketing sales of his products in the last decade emerged with the advent of Starbucks and other North American coffee shops.

Italian-sounding names of men's and women's clothiers, fine leather shoes and so many other luxe items from cologne to home design have become part of our common language. Names such as Armani, Prada, Dolce & Gabbana and Gucci come to us from Milan's and Rome's runways, but the Italian Canadian names of Civello, Marc Anthony and Lou Myles are also well known. In addition, Italian model Linda Evangelista and singer Michael Bublé have given Italian Canadians a look and a voice that is strictly Italian Canadian.

If you took a double take when I mentioned Michael Bublé, don't worry. I did too the first time I heard he was Italian. "Bublé" is not a typical Italian name. Michael was born in Burnaby, BC, to an Italian family. His father is from Abruzzo, while his mother comes from Veneto. Michael's love of jazz came from his *nonno* (grandpa) Santagata. He knew he wanted to be a singer and to sing the songs his grandfather loved so much. It was perhaps the warm rapport his Italian grandfather extended to him that fuelled Michael's passion for his famous crooner-style love songs.

If Michael Bublé's CDs are at the top of the charts in Canada and in Italy, it's just another Italy-Canada love affair. In his article about Little Italys, Gabriele Scardellato describes the way in which film producer

Jerry Ciccoritti uses language as poetry to depict unforgettable moments and scenes. He says that "Ciccoritti presents Italian-language poetry in film as the language of love that makes possible a romance between a Canadian boy and an Italian girl" apt metaphors for Canada and Italy. He continues to explain: "Canada meets and falls in love with Italy in a romance that overcomes language and the barriers to understanding and integration that it can symbolize. In other words, for the second and subsequent generations of Italian Canadians, Little Italy, with its bars, restaurants and other venues, has become a site for romantic encounters. All suggestions of threat posed by the immigrant *other* has dissipated just as the immigrant language itself no longer signifies argument: rather, it has become an essential ingredient for love and romance."

Italians have reached fame not only through the quality of their products but also by making a name for themselves and attaining success in politics, sports, media, business, art and literature. Below is a recent list of Italian Canadians, from Wikipedia, who have achieved fame in various types of endeavours:

Dominic Agostino (1959–2004)—Ontario politician
Maria Augimeri—Toronto city councillor
Mario Adamo—prominent Toronto businessman and owner
   of Verdi Hospitality Centre and Hockley Valley Resort
Marisa Ferretti Barth—Senator
Rick Bartolucci—Ontario politician
Lorenzo Berardinetti—Ontario politician
Mario Bernardi—Conductor and pianist
Todd Bertuzzi—NHL player
Maurizio Bevilacqua—Federal politician
Michael Bublé—Singer

Dave Bidini—Musician and writer

Adolfo Bresciano (a.k.a. Dino Bravo) (1948–93)—Professional wrestler

Italo Brutto—Commissioner of Engineering and Public Works in Richmond Hill

Charles Caccia—Former politician

Pietro Calendino—British Columbia politician

Rick Campanelli—Television personality

Luigi Giovanni Vitale Cappello (1843–1902)—Painter

Deanna Casaluce—Television actress in *Degrassi: The Next Generation*

Anna-Marie Castrilli—Ontario politician

Carlo Onorato Catelli (1849–1937)—Businessman and founder of Catelli Pasta in 1867

Bob Chiarelli—Mayor of Ottawa

Peter Chiarelli—Manager of the Boston Bruins

Rick Chiarelli—Ottawa city councillor

Rita Chiarelli—Blues singer

Hayden Christensen—Actor

John Ciaccia—Former Québec politician

Enrico Colantoni—Actor

Mike Colle—Ontario politician

Joe Comuzzi—Politician

Joseph Cordiano—Ontario politician

Paulo Costanzo—Actor

Bobby Curtola—Musician

Scott D'Amore—Professional wrestler

Yvonne De Carlo—Actress

Anne Marie De Cicco—Mayor of London, Ontario

Pierre-Charles de Liette (1697–1749)—Colonial army officer in New France and Louisiana

Giuseppe De Natale—Kickboxer

Alex Delvecchio—NHL Player

Thomas Delvecchio (1758–1826)—Businessman

Pier Giorgio Di Cicco—Poet, Toronto Poet Laureate, Curator of the Toronto Museum Project and Global Centre for Cities

Caroline Di Cicco—Ontario politician

Larry Di Ianni—Mayor of Hamilton

Elio Di Iorio—Ontario municipal politician

Primo Di Luca—Past president of The Famee Furlane in Toronto

Mary Di Michele—Writer and poet

Consiglio Di Nino—Senator

Patrizia Di Sciascio—Senior art director for Wunderman/Rogers Media & Communications; Canadian Representative for Art Direction in Bruxelles and Munich Global Summits

Odoardo Di Santo—Ontario politician

Melissa Di Marco—Actress

Nick Discepola—Politician

John Anthony Donegani (1798–1868)—Businessman and seigneur

Angelo Esposito—NHL player

Phil Esposito—NHL player

Tony Esposito—NHL goalie

Linda Evangelista—Supermodel

Lara Fabian—Singer

Julian Fantino—Former Toronto police chief

Gerome Fassio (1789–1851)—Artist

Giuseppe Fava—Producer of *That Night at the Opera*, Canada's oldest Italian music radio program

Adrian Ferrazzutti—Artist

Joe Fontana—Politician

John Forzani—Businessman and former CFL player

Joe Fratesi—Former mayor of Sault Ste. Marie

Freeway Frank—Canadian radio personality

Liza Frulla—Politician

Rick Fuschi—Conservative Party of Canada activist

Philip Gagliardi (1913–95)—British Columbia politician

Arturo Gatti—Professional boxer

Alfonso Gagliano—Former Minister of Foreign Policy

Ken Georgetti—Labour leader

Bruno Gerussi (1928–95)—Actor

Adam Giambrone—Toronto city councillor and NDP Party activist

Frank, Ralph, Antonietta, & Mariana Giannone—from the FRAM Construction group (architectural builders of environment friendly and energy-saving homes)

Giuseppe Gori—Ontario politician

Jessica Grassia—Musician in The Golden Dogs

Albina Guarnieri—Politician

Frank Iacobucci—Former Supreme Court of Canada Justice

Tony Ianno—Politician

Alessandro Juliani—Voice actor

Bob Lenarduzzi—Soccer player and coach

Laureano Leone—Former Ontario politician

Peter Li Preti—Toronto city councillor

Johnny Lombardi (1915–2002)—Broadcasting executive

Carmen Lombardo (1902–77)—Musician and band leader

Roberto Luongo—NHL goalie

Giorgio Mammoliti—Ontario politician

Mark Mancari—NHL player

Nick Mancuso—Actor

Anthony S. Manera—Former CBC president

Rosario Marchese—Ontario politician

Sergio Marchi—Politician

Pat Mastroianni—Actor

Bill Mauro—Ontario politician

Diego G. Mazzone—Sales management professional

Domenico Mazzone Jr.—Politician and radio talk-show host

Maria Minna—Politician

Misstress Barbara—Disc jockey
Guido Molinari (1933–2004)—Artist
Sergio Momesso—NHL player
Joe Morsèlli—Québec businessman
Guido Nincheri (1885–1973)—Artist
Frances Nunziata—Toronto city councillor
John Nunziata—Politician
Massimo Pacetti—Politician
Al Palladini (1943–2001)—Politician
Joe Pantalone—Toronto deputy mayor
Sarina Paris—Singer
Gianna Patriarca—Poet
Anthony Perruzza—Ontario politician
Joe Peschisolido—Politician
Angelo Pienovi (1773–1845)—Painter
Damiano Pietropaolo—Producer at CBC Radio
Fernando Pisani—NHL player
Claudio Polsinelli—Former Ontario politician
Carly Pope—Actress
Carmen Provenzano (1942–2005)—Politician
Sandra Pupatello—Ontario politician
Rick Ravanello—Actor
Mark Recchi—NHL player
Karen Redman—Politician
Nino Ricci—Writer
Michele Rigali (1841–1910)—Sculptor
Tony Rizzo—Ontario politician
Pietro Rizzuto (1934–97)—Businessman and senator
Anthony Rota—Politician
Adamo Ruggiero –Television actor in *Degrassi: The Next
    Generation*
Ivana Santilli—Singer
Lino Saputo—Businessman and billionaire
Johnny Saputo—Radio DJ at KREB

Will Sasso—Actor and comedian
Ray Scapinello—NHL player
Francis Scarpaleggia—Politician
Mario Sergio—Ontario politician
Tony Silipo—Former Ontario politician
Greg Sorbara—Ontario politician
Martina Sorbara—Singer and songwriter
Jean-Fernand Spagnolini (1704–64)—Physician in New
    France
Jason Spezza—NHL player
Rick Tocchet—NHL player
Henri de Tonti (1659–1727)—Explorer in New France
Anna Maria Tremonti—Journalist and CBC Radio
    announcer
Domenic Troiano (1946–2005)—Musician
Marty Turco—NHL goalie
Michael Vadacchino—Politician
Tony Valeri—Politician
Gino Vannelli—Musician
Joe Volpe—Politician
Giuliano Zaccardelli—Former commissioner of the RCMP

CHAPTER FOURTEEN

ITALIAN CANADIANS ON THE WORLD STAGE

In a nation of immigrants they have made an incredible contribution to both the social fabric of the country and the Canadian economy.
–Lindsay Gordon, president and CEO of
HSBC Bank of Canada

Today Canada is experiencing strong economic growth. It has been ranked as one of the countries with the highest standards of living worldwide and as one of the best fiscally managed in the G8. One of the reasons for this is that Canada has adopted new policies in international investment. In our present global economy, Canadian and foreign investment are key international business strategies of both the Government of Canada and Canadian industry. This means that countries from around the globe are investing in Canadian industries, while Canada is also investing in other countries' products.

International trade agreements are an integral part of globalization. Companies in Toronto can do business with any city in the world. Especially via the Internet, there are no more national borders. Not only can we do business with the world, but we can also share ideas, information and entertainment. Canadians and people from all over the globe are brought together by television, phone, e-mail and text messages. Because of this, the world's cultures are virtually as close to us as our own. This, of course, includes the Italian culture.

In a speech in Rome, Italy, on January 25, 2000, the Honourable John Manley explained: "between the years 1988 and 1998, Italian investment in Canada has seen an increase of $343 million, bringing total investment in Canada to $672 million. This makes Italy Canada's 14th-largest source of direct foreign investment." Not bad for a trading partner that has also been ranked high in the G8—in fifth place. "Partnership" is the key word, and this partnership has been facilitated not only by the government's agenda but also by the thousands of entrepreneurs who have made it their livelihood to import and export products in all areas of business.

Canada is a major player in the global market, not only because of large companies like Nortel or Teleglobe but also because of smaller enterprises, of which Italian Canadians hold quite a share. In a 2005 publication from the Italian Chamber of Commerce in Toronto, entitled *Made in Canada: The Italian Way,* author Corrado Paina showcases the success stories of today's top Canadian entrepreneurs of Italian origin. These are business leaders who, according to Ron

Sedran, vice-president of Canaccord Capital, "have made meaningful cultural, professional and artistic contributions throughout their careers" for the betterment of Canada. Theirs are stories of perseverance, strong community support, skill, daring and creative innovation. They have overcome many obstacles, from moving to a new country, learning a new language and starting businesses that today are crossing national borders.

Since their arrival in Canada, Italian immigrants have been ambassadors of Italian culture and products. Nivo Angelone, president of the Italian Chamber of Commerce in Toronto, explains how "throughout the 1900s Italian culture spread throughout the world." The many success stories of business endeavours by Italian Canadians are proof that they have indeed played a part in shaping Canada's economy. Their efforts are not only important within our country's borders, but they have had an impact globally.

Perhaps one of the most notable entrepreneurs of Italian origin in Canada is Richard Lovat. The son of a miner, Lovat was always aware of the dangers of mining, especially because he lost his father at a young age because of silicosis, a lung disease associated with working in mines. His father's death drove Richard to eventually create his world-renowned company, Lovat Inc. in the early '70s. When he first arrived in Canada, Richard Lovat worked in construction jobs, excavating tunnels in dangerous conditions. He saw the flaws in the construction safety system and ingeniously designed machines that could make working conditions safer. Mr. Lovat invented the "Talpa" (which translates as "mole"), a tunnel-boring machine, and that was the beginning of his incredible success. His

Mining in northern Ontario (1918).

company was the first to manufacture the machine, and the Talpa was soon purchased by all other excavating companies to replace their old methods of digging tunnels with the use of compressed air. Tunnel-boring machines are used in mining and excavation sites throughout Canada today. They are also exported worldwide, with the U.S. being the largest market.

Another Italian Canadian success story is that of Michael Mosca, senior vice-president and chief operating officer of Equinox Films. On the roster of some of the well-known films produced by his company are *My Fat Greek Wedding*, *Mambo Italiano*, *Kamouraska*, *The Three Madeleines* and *Seraphim: Heart of Stone*. Mosca's film production company was also responsible for the distribution of *The Passion of the Christ*. He is strongly attached to his roots and believes that

Italian culture has had a huge impact on Canadian culture. He stands behind his company in producing films that reflect the sociopsychological issues of the Italian community.

The successes of Italian Canadians in both the national and global economy run through every facet of industry, business, science, politics and the arts. Below is a list of Italian Canadians showcased in *Made in Canada: The Italian Way.* They are not the only success stories, as there are many thousands more throughout Canada. They are just a small representation of Italian Canadians who have influenced Canada's economy.

Walter Arbib—CEO of Skylink Aviation

Eugene Barone—Entrepreneur

Elisabetta Bigsby—Senior executive, vice-president of Human Resources and Public Affairs at RBC Financial

Gianni Bragagnolo—President of Albatours International

Daniel Brambilla—CEO of the Hummingbird Centre

Rudolph Bratty—Partner of Bratty and Partners

Tony Cianciotta—President of Capri Releasing

Dominic D'Alessandro—President and CEO of Manulife Financial

Fred De Gasperis—President of Con Drain Company Group

Nick Di Donato—President, Liberty Entertainment Group

Sam Di Michele—Executive vice-president and general manager for Canada Cineplex Odeon

Consiglio Di Nino—Senator in the Government of Canada

Peter Donolo—Executive vice-president of The Strategic Council

Frank Falvo—President of Falco Steel Fabrications Inc.

Gaetano Gagliano—Chairman and founder of St. Joseph Corporation

Dan Iannuzzi—President of Multicom Media

Angelo Locilento—President of Cilento Wines

Richard Lovat—Chairman of Lovat Inc.

Joseph Mancinelli—International vice-president and regional manager of the Labour's International Union of North America (LIUNA) for central and eastern Canada

Norberto Marocco—President of Shade-o-Matic

Gabriella Martinelli—President of Capri Films

Gesualdo Mastruzzo—President of Numage Trading Inc.

Michael Mosca—Senior vice-president & CEO of Equinox Films

Steven Muzzo—President of OZZ Corporation

Paolo Palamara—President of Diamante Development Corporation

Arturo Pelliccione—Owner of Jan K. Overweel Ltd.

Franco Prevedello—Entrepreneur

Gina Scola—Vice-president of Investment Services at Goodman Private Wealth Management

Sergio Sgaramella—Publisher of *Azure* magazine

Joseph Vitale—President of Italpasta Ltd.

Giuseppe Zanchin—President of Zanchin Auto Group

Donald Ziraldo—Managing director and co-founder of Inniskillin Wines Inc.

Today, Toronto is Canada's largest, most influential city that has made an excellent reputation for itself not only within Canada, but also on the world stage. The city's proximity to the U.S. makes it an ideal gateway to North America. Toronto is a multicultural, cosmopolitan city much ahead of many modern cities in its role of promoting a dynamic sense of opportunity, growth and innovation. Its many immigrants make it a hub of cultures and ideas and provide the city with a cultural and business edge, by creating connections to the many countries where they originated. Because of these links, Canada has established beneficial alliances with European and world leaders in many, varied fields. The mayor of Toronto, David Miller, for example, has tried to revitalize the economic development of the city, making good use of the wishes of its citizens and gaining input from city planners of other successful city centres such as Milan, Berlin and London. In one of his speeches, Miller expressed the idea of Toronto transforming into "the, cultural capital of the 21st century." He aims to do this through partnerships with foreign cities that have the same goals.

If in the last few decades Italians in Canada have held manual labour jobs, today we see a definite shift. The children of Italian immigrants have integrated into the social fabric of this country. Many of them have felt compelled to achieve higher goals in order to make their parents' sacrifices worthwhile. Joe Pantalone was one such young person. Having emigrated with his family from southern Italy, Joe was 13 years old when he arrived in Canada. He "found a home and a community that was vibrant, diverse, somewhat daunting and yet welcoming."

Joe is currently the deputy mayor of Toronto. Before this post, he served the community for 26 years as city councillor. He was responsible for leading the revitalization of Exhibition Place into a showcase of renewable energy and was the chair of Exhibition Place and vice-chair of the city's executive committee. He has also been a member of Tourism Toronto board of directors and the executive of the Toronto's Economic Development Corporation.

Adam Giambrone is another city councillor of Italian background. As one of the youngest and most dynamic members of Toronto's city council, Giambrone also serves as chair of the Toronto Transit Commission. Pantalone and Giambrone are just a few examples of the many Italian Canadians who are working for the success and improvement of our communities.

Italians came to Canada as labourers and industry workers. Many times they had to fight the obstacles of prejudice and stereotype. In spite of it all, they persevered. As Toronto's former chief of police, Julian Fantino, so eloquently said, "I had to deal with racist slurs in my career as a police officer in Toronto. The way I dealt with it was not to respond, not to focus on it, but to forge ahead with my goals and to prove them wrong."

It is perhaps what many successful people do: focus their energy on worthwhile goals, minimizing the negativity, thus weakening it. Overall, the entrepreneurial contributions of Italian Canadians to the success of the Canadian economy are indisputable. From the import-export ventures of companies such as Faema, Vespa, Dorgel, Varese, Pirelli, Ferrari, to the companies created in Canada by Italian Canadians, such as Italpasta, Vin Bon, Trimatrix and countless others, we have all gained both culturally and financially, because of their efforts. With an eye to the past and one on the future, Italian Canadians have held on to the quality and craftsmanship of their traditional family businesses, creating products we can all love and relate to.

CHAPTER FIFTEEN

ITALIAN CANADIANS CHANGING THE FACE OF CANADIAN CULTURE THROUGH THE ARTS

Italian Canadian writing expresses the contrasts and connections between Italy and Canada, often fusing the authors' Italian and Canadian identities. Italian Canadian writers attempt to balance material and spiritual values as they speak of the price their parents, often labourers, paid for success in Canada.
–The Canadian Encyclopedia Historica: Ethnic Writing

Perhaps at the pinnacle of a people's culture is the artistic legacy that they leave behind for future generations: what remains to tell the world that they have been here and had an influence. Perhaps most important of all, is the historical and literary documentation of a given culture.

From the dawn of their immigration to Canada, Italians were instrumental in beautifying and decorating churches and government buildings. The wonderful infrastructures of roadways and cityscapes that we all take for granted as always having been there were built by hardworking Italians. Italian products were introduced to Canada through the particular interests of Italian business people. Such imports have beautified and improved so many facets of our everyday life with innovations in style and lifestyle that their mark is felt in all areas of Canadian life. These include fashion design, home decor, beauty and hairstyling, cafés and restaurants, food products, popular recipes, music, media and film, our new national interest in soccer and a growing respect for all Italian products.

The increased awareness of Italian quality, lifestyle and Italians' penchant for beautiful things was showcased at the 2004 "Presenza" Exhibit in Ottawa and also at "Italian Design Week" held in Toronto at the Royal Ontario Museum in 2006. What used to be of interest only to Italian Canadians has now become of cultural interest to mainstream Canada.

Italian Canadians have become self-aware of their identity within the Canadian context. They are writing about their experiences and showcasing them through literature, theatre and film. In spite of many famous Italian Canadians, such as Giovanni Caboto, Guglielmo Marconi, musician Guy Lombardo, hockey star Alec Del Vecchio and federal judge Franc Iacobucci, most contributions of Italian Canadians have been nameless. In *Canadese: A Portrait of Italian Canadians*, Kenneth Bagnell states: "there may be value, especially for the young, to look with pride to the pantheon of the Italian contribution in Canada, but the history of Italian Canadians is not the story of the famous, but of solid citizens on ordinary streets."

The presence of these regular citizens is what has had a tangible influence on Canadian life. Writers, artists and filmmakers are writing about these people and their experiences, adding their stories to the bulk of Canadian literary culture, which thus far had excluded them. Italian Canadians had, until a few decades ago, been what playwright Marco Micone called them in one of his plays, the "Voiceless People."

Italians, like all other peoples arriving on our shores, have always kept diaries and records of their experiences. Giovanni Caboto himself, in 1497, wrote of his first encounter with Canadian soil in his captain's log. Following him were other explorers, such as Verrazzano, who recorded Canada's new territories in their geographical descriptions of the New World. Perhaps the first true writer in the midst of the first wave of explorers and settlers in Canada was Francesco Giuseppe Bressani, the Jesuit missionary, stationed in New France from 1642 to 1650. He wrote a long description of Canada and its Native people from an Italian perspective. The work became part of a larger work in French entitled *The Jesuit Relations*, translated from the original Latin version *Breve Relatione*. But even at this point, we cannot really speak of Italian Canadian writing as an actual literature. At best it was a documentation of events and experiences.

Many artists, poets and performers arrived in Canada after the first settlements, though most of these people were travellers who didn't see themselves as part of a new literature or artistic movement. They wrote accounts of what they saw, and many of them returned home to Italy. Like Guglielmo Marconi, who launched his telegraph messages for the first time from Canada's east coast, they came to Canada as adventurers.

But some came to avoid prosecution. In 1842 Carlo Antonio Napoleone Gallenga, an Italian from Parma, had to change his name to Louis Mariotti and escape from Italy for his involvement with the political ideas of Italian, revolutionary leader Giuseppe Mazzini. In order to escape the attention of the police of his native city, he left Parma for Canada and became the first teacher of Italian in the country, at Windsor's King's College, in Nova Scotia.

It wasn't until 1853 that the University of Toronto created its first courses of Italian language and literature. The first chairman of Italian Studies at the University of Toronto was professor Giacomo Forneri, an Italian intellectual from Racconigi, in Piemonte. He had been a former Italian soldier in the Napoleonic wars and then a teacher in Italy, in Britain and eventually in Canada. Forneri was the most famous among the teachers of Italian studies at the University of Toronto.

Two poets, Liborio Lattoni and Francesco Gualtieri, wrote *We Italians: A Study in Italian Immigration in Canada* in 1928 and are briefly mentioned in Canadian literary history. Also, an Italian journalist named Mario Duliani came to Montréal in 1936 as a writer for *La Presse*. He later wrote an account of the experiences of Italian men interned at Camp Petawawa, while he himself was imprisoned there. His book was called *The City Without Women*.

In spite of many attempts that people of Italian origin made to write about their experiences, they were sporadic, faint attempts, which never received much recognition. Their work comprised a fringe body of literature that never made it as a part of mainstream Canadian literature.

Perhaps one can only begin to speak of a true Italian Canadian literature in the '60s and '70s when groups of Italian writers began to congregate in Toronto and Montréal. They were the sons and daughters of Italian immigrants who had come after the war, and because they were educated in Canada, they became the first writers who wrote about what it felt like to be Italian in a Canadian context.

A true movement of Italian Canadian literature then, can be said to have begun with Pier Giorgio Di Cicco in 1975. A prolific poet himself and editor of the Ontario literary magazine, *Books in Canada,* Di Cicco discovered that there were a number of Italian writers across the country who were writing and having their work published. Di Cicco was nominated Toronto's Poet Laureate in 2004 for his contribution to contemporary Canadian literature. He was the first writer of Italian origin to create a body of work that dealt with the state of consciousness of Italian Canadians. He founded the first group of Italian Canadian writers in Toronto and is recognized as the father of Italian Canadian writing. Today, The Italian Canadian Writers Association comprises thousands of members throughout Canada, Europe and the United States. It has influenced the thought of mainstream Canadian literary discourse by intersecting it, along with other ethnic writings, with a unique sense of perspective. These writers deal with the universal themes of language, alienation, family, loss and identity, but above all, they have created literature with heart.

Through their art, whether poetry, novels or plays, Italian writers reflected and expressed their identity. Some of these include Mary Di Michele, Maria Ardizzi, Frank Paci, Joseph Pivato, Fulvio Caccia, and Antonino

Mazza. *Roman Candles* was the first anthology of Italian Canadian writing compiled and edited by Pier Giorgio Di Cicco. It was the beginning of what was to become a new self-awareness about Italian Canadian identity within Canadian literature.

Other writers soon followed suit: Frank Paci, Marco Micone, Antonio D'Alfonso, Mary Melfi, Filippo Salvatore and many more. In 1979, Antonio D'Alfonso founded the publishing house Guernica Editions in Montréal. It eventually moved to Toronto where it has established itself as the major Italian Canadian North American press, finally giving voice to Italian Canadian talent. Today, Guernica publishes all talented Canadian authors, regardless of ethnicity. The quality of the work, not ethnic affiliation, is what is important.

Many anthologies and novels have been published by Italian Canadians since '70s. The birth of a true Italian Canadian literature has prompted many conferences, symposiums and book launchings with Italian Canadian writers across Canada and worldwide.

The same can be said for film and theatre. Having had access to higher education and unbound by the economic pressures of their parents, many young playwrights and filmmakers are beginning to express their own as well as their parents' experiences. Marco Micone, one of Canada's best playwrights of Italian background, tries to give Italian people living in Canada a voice, which he believes, until recently, they didn't have. Through visual representation, people see themselves on stage, as they are, as they sound, and are thus able to become self-aware. It is here, at this point, that Micone wants to bring them, so that they can begin to understand themselves. But Micone is not the only one to work with the medium of theatre in order to give a voice to Italians living in Canada.

The themes of family, marriage, religion and language and all circumstances related to them, are explored by playwrights such as Caterina Edwards, Mary Melfi, Frank Canino, Tony Nardi and Charly Chiarelli. Their plays speak to us of struggles with race and culture, their parents' pain of loss of their motherland and touch on the existence of people at the margins of society. Most of these playwrights often use a mix of English, Italian and dialect of both languages to create their characters. This method of writing reflects the reality of Italian Canadians true-to-life existence, in which one or a mix of all three languages is usually spoken. This hybrid language usually evokes laughter from Italian audiences. It invites people to laugh at themselves by illustrating the truth of many life situations and giving the audience a chance to look at themselves as they truly are and not as they imagine themselves to be.

Italian Canadian theatre is thriving, with many more young playwrights emerging not only in Toronto and Montréal but also throughout the country. Theatre gives a voice to all Canadians, who through such representations can identify and relate with issues of their own ethnic backgrounds. Through the metaphors of poetry and the images of theatre and film, we are given the opportunity to be profoundly touched, and we are often changed.

With their medium, Canadian filmmakers of Italian heritage have also contributed much to Canadian cinema. The last 10 years have especially seen many talented directors arrive on the film stage. These include Jerry Ciccoritti, Paul Tana, Vincenzo Natali,

Steve Galluccio and Derek Diorio, just to name a few. Nino Ricci's famous novel *The Lives of the Saints* aired on national television in 2006 as one of CTV's best Canadian made-for-TV movies in 2006. Directed by Jerry Ciccoritti, the movie recounted the fictional tale of one Italian Canadian family and starred Sophia Loren with Italian Canadian actor Nick Mancuso.

On September 8, 2004, a new film festival was added to Montréal's already impressive list of film festivals. "Quintus," Montréal's first Italian Film Festival, was founded by Joe Sisto and Dino Mazzone, who named the festival after a famous Roman actor, Quintus Roscius Gallus (126–62 BC). The film festival was held at the Leonardo da Vinci Community Centre in Montréal's Little Italy on St. Leonard Street. The festival ran for five days, and it screened 32 films from around the world. All of the films had to have either themes related to Italian culture and society or had to have been produced by people of Italian heritage. The festival's main objective is to promote Italian culture and to support filmmakers who want to broach Italian themes within the larger Canadian and global culture.

This festival is unique because it does not limit its film entries only to Italian language films. Many films showcased at Quintus have since appeared either in Canadian theatres or on television. Some of the most well-known titles include *Ciao Bella*, *Mambo Italiano*, *Capo Nord*, *Mostly Martha*, *Pontormo*, *Qualcosa*, *Passato Prossimo*, *Prisoners Among Us*, *Aspiration* and *Looking for Angelina*.

One of the most prolific Italian Canadian filmmakers is Paul Tana. He arrived in Montréal from Italy when he was 11 years old. He graduated from university with a degree in literature. It was in university that he began making student films, although at that time, he hadn't received formal training in filmmaking. Because of his interest in film, he joined l'Association Cooperative de Production Audio-Visuelle in Montréal. Today his films are shown in Canada, Italy and around the world. Some of his well-known successes include *La Deroute*, *La Sarrasine*, *Cube*, *The Life Before This* and *Caffe Italia*, which he made with the collaboration of author Bruno Ramirez.

Tana attributes the success of his movies to them coming at "a time when the majority of society was discovering the 'other,' the immigrant, no matter what origin, Italian, Greek, Iraqi." One only has to think of the impact *My Big Fat Greek Wedding* had on all of us. It didn't matter that it was about a Greek girl marrying a Canadian guy. As Canadians, we could all identify with its themes.

Author and publisher Antonio D'Alfonso comments on a 1996 Statistics Canada report in which Italian Canadians are said to be among the most affluent groups in the population. He believes that more could be done culturally and academically. "The only future our children will know is what we leave behind in books, music and art. And that comes from education and schooling and serious community and cultural life."

In the end, it is the educated person who will be better equipped to navigate through the ever more complicated and specialized web of the future. Knowledge and pride in one's history will be the springboard from which to leap, the first step into a wider path of learning.

Springing from the basic human needs of food and shelter, many immigrants, including the Italians, have left their countries to give their families a better future. But as the old Italian proverb says, "non si vive di solo pane" (man doesn't live by bread alone). From the plethora of academic programs, books, films, television programs, art and music being produced by Italian Canadians today, we can see that this is certainly the case.

CHAPTER SIXTEEN

THE FUTURE OF ITALIAN CANADIANS

Resistance is futile: prepare to be assimilated.
–The Borg, *Star Trek: The Next Generation*

One day I will lose my mother. Just the thought of it fills me with tears and heartache. She is my strongest link with my Italian past. Besides being my mother and my best friend, she has taught me everything I know about life, taking me, as the song says, from crayons to perfume, to learning how to write neatly, to colouring within the lines, embroidering, sewing, knitting, cooking, baking, gardening and all manner of traditions. She is my personal repository of proverbs, old family stories and family information that will be lost forever when she is no longer here. The tales she told my sister and I will be forever etched in my memory. There was always a pervasive sadness to her stories, although she tried to spice them up with humour or sarcasm. The sadness of her voice and the tragedy in the stories seeped through.

I often wonder how she did it. How she could leave her own family and her life to move away with us across the ocean as she did. All those airmail letters and brief long-distance phone calls with the long pauses in between because of bad reception, and the tears, all those sobs I heard her cry when her mother, then her sister, died. Throughout the years, I thought my mother was invincible. No matter what happened, she always carried on. I learned from her to keep on working even when things are bad. Maybe that was an Italian thing to do. There were cookies to bake, gardens to tend to, groceries to be bought and laundry to be washed and ironed. The sad conversations and all the physical discomforts she underwent, which I mistook for typical Italian drama when I was young, I now comprehend as the tragic threads of a heart breaking, like my heart will, when she will no longer be here. The worst thing is that I don't know how I'll handle it. Without her hand to hold me rooted in my past, the steep cliff of the future will undoubtedly swallow up what remains of me, and my sons, too, into the unknown landscape of assimilation.

Everyone's ultimate fear is the fear of death. Annihilation is what one fears when one thinks of assimilation: the death of self, of one's unique identity. Of course, one has larger fish to fry on a day-to-day basis. But it is a malaise that sits on the backburner of perception of every immigrant who has had to redefine one's identity in a different culture.

One of the surest ways to lose your identity is to lose your language. This is usually followed by loss of customs, which progresses to an eventual loss of culture. It is fear that propels people of every ethnicity to seek others of similar background with whom to share their language and beliefs. It is what has kept Québec struggling for independence and cultural survival within the borders of English Canada and the social anxiety that has plagued every ethnic group not belonging to the dominant culture of our country. Interestingly, it is the same fear that English Canadians feel at the thought of being overwhelmed by immigration from every corner of the world, thus losing the old parameters of what it looked like to be Canadian. Without language and traditions, people become one with the host culture and soon assimilate. This basically means that they become indistinguishable from the rest. It spells cultural death.

Is this fear based in truth? Is it unfounded? A perfect example is that of the Italian immigrants in the United States. They have been there much longer than Italians have been in Canada. Many of them are now third- and fourth-generation Italian Americans. Many have intermarried and are proud Americans. They have successfully assimilated into the American melting pot. Or have they?

In spite of the "melting pot" metaphor, and in spite of centuries of assimilation, Italian Americans still seem to retain a distinct cultural identity. They have Italian names and have kept Italian organizations and clubs. Despite the loss of language, they have maintained Italian customs, so to speak. They have retained their mannerisms and ways of living and loving that are so uniquely Italian. Many of them are professionals, politicians, actors, producers, authors, professors and so on. Rudolph Giuliani, the former mayor of New

York, is Italian. Although fiercely American, he is also proud of being Italian.

So, what kind of future is there for Italians after assimilation? What kind of future is there for any culture in the process of assimilation? In today's global village, identity is becoming once again a personal, localized issue. Identity is becoming stronger in a strange way. No longer is there a need to feel affiliated to a nationality per se. On the worldwide web of our Internet world, who we are is essential only in as much as we can relate to others who are just like ourselves. We can find them here in Canada, in our village in Italy or anywhere else on the planet. We are no longer bound by the restrictions of country borders. We are encouraged to seek out people like ourselves and to share our commonalities with them.

Over the many decades of immigration and settlement in Canada, Italians have created social networks that extend into every facet of life. Newspapers, radio, television, cinema, theatre, schools, churches and community centres all give Italian Canadians a strong sense of connection and identity. They have established their own retirement centres, such as "Villa Colombo"; their own social aid centres, such as "COSTI; their own dance halls; their own newspapers, such as *Corriere Canadese/Tandem*; and OMNI television, TELELATINO and 'RAI INTERNATIONAL. Italian Canadians have business associations, such as the CIBPA, and are involved at every level of government. Italian Canadians also represent their people as authors, with what has been described as the highest quality of Italian writing outside of Italy. We can definitely say that Italians have integrated into the Canadian culture.

Derrick de Kerckhove, in his study of Italian Canadian identity, explains that cultural identity can be identified by several factors, among which are food, music, art, literature, architecture, city neighbourhoods, language, dialects, colloquial expressions, jokes, common gathering places, political affiliation and representation, community, celebrations and rituals, religion and attachment and connection to the motherland. Italian identity within Canada can be well measured by these elements. It is easy to assume that if these conditions continue to exist and are nurtured by future generations of Italian Canadians, the identity of these people will not disappear, but who can say for sure.

Voicelessness is what has spurred me and people like me to write accounts about the presence and the accomplishments of Italian Canadians in Canada. It is important to document the contributions and successes, perhaps not only for Italian Canadians themselves but also for other Canadians. Without such historical resources, we would remain unaware of the large numbers of people who for centuries have lived in, worked in and created the Canada we have all come to know.

Canada is experiencing a similar identity crisis with the large number of people entering its borders from all over the world. The familiar is changed. Variety replaces the monochromatic sameness of the past. But perhaps homogeneity is only an illusion if we delve deeper into the history of our country. The influx of a myriad cultures has always been at the foundation of our land. The paradox of culture is that although it appears static, it is transient and ever changing, as it is constantly influenced by other customs and traditions it comes in contact with.

In the same way that languages over time have vanished or morphed into new ones, cultures also leave a mark on the thought, lifestyle and history of the world they come in contact with. As the permeable membranes of Canada's various, multiple ways of life blend into one another, we gain a mixture of flavours, ideas, histories, creativity and ultimately, a new, unparalleled depth of culture. Italian culture is only one component of the mix.

Integration then, not alienation, is the hope of Italians and all people living in Canada. Identity can be somewhat preserved, although forever enriched by contact with other cultures. We can be a global model of what it means to co-exist culturally, if we remember that everyone else in the world is dealing with such issues, including host societies. Within their families and their communities, Italians will certainly continue to exist as uniquely so, even though thoroughly Canadian. As the motto of Dan Iannuzzi's *Corriere Canadese* newspaper so clearly expresses, they have the freedom to be "Proudly Italian, but Fiercely Canadian."

NOTES ON SOURCES

Albi Davies, Adriana. "Italian Community and the Heritage Community Foundation." 2006. http://www.albertasource.ca/abitalian/background/rockies_cb_pioneers_crowsnest3.html

Alnirabie, Fuad, and Michael Vesia. "An Interview with Paul Tana." http://www.horschamp.qc.ca/new_offscreen/Tana.html. Offscreen Editorial Essay: 2001.

"Antonio Meucci." http://freemasonry.bcy.ca/biography/meucci_a/meucci_a.html

Bagnell, Kenneth. *Canadese: A Portrait of the Italian Canadians.* Toronto: MacMillan of Canada, 1989.

Barber, John. "Legendary Developer Dies After 55-Year Career." *The Globe and Mail,* December 7, 2005.

Broadfoot, Barry. *The Pioneer Years 1895–1914.* Toronto: Doubleday Canada, 1976.

Buzzelli, Michael. "From Little Britain to Little Italy: An Urban Ethnic Landscape Study in Toronto." *Journal of Historical Geography,* 27, 4. Academic Press. School of Geography and Geology. Hamilton, ON: McMaster University. 2001.

Carbone, Stanislao. *Italians in Winnipeg: An Illustrated History.* Winnipeg: University of Manitoba Press, 1998.

CHIN Radio. "Johnny Lombardi." http://www.chinradio.com/jlombardi.php

Costa, Elio. Quote from Antonio Maglio's Article, "How Multiculturalism Was Born." Toronto: Tandem. November 27, 2003.

Crupi, Carmelina. "Stereotypes Sell–But We're Not for Sale." http://www.ginavalle.com

Culos, Ray. "Michael Bublé. Si e Canadese, But his Roots Are Italian!" *Accenti,* Summer 2006.

D'Alfonso, Antonio. *In Italics: In Defence of Ethnicity.* Toronto: Guernica, 1996.

De Klerck, Denis, and Corrado Paina. *College Street, Little Italy.* Toronto: Mansfield Press, 2006.

Del Negro, Giovanna. *Looking Through My Mother's Eyes.* Montreal: Guernica Editions, 1997.

Di Giovanni, Caroline Morgan. *Italian Canadian Voices.* (Nocturne by Mario Duliani.) Oakville: Mosaic Press, 1984.

Donaldson, Gordon. *Fifteen Men: Canada's Prime Ministers from MacDonald to Trudeau.* Toronto: Doubleday Canada, 1969.

Fanella, Antonella. "Italian Pioneers in Western Canada." *Accenti,* Winter, 2006.

Fantino, Julian. Quotes from Antonio Maglio's article, "How Multiculturalism Was Born When Rights and Laws Began to Benefit Italian Immigrants Who Faced Hardships." Toronto: Tandem, November 27, 2003.

Friuli Benevolent Corporation. *Landed: A Pictorial Mosaic of Friulani Immigration to Canada.* Toronto: Friesen Printers, 1992.

Harney, Robert. *If One Were to Write a History.* Toronto: The Multicultural History Society of Ontario, 1991.

Harney, Robert. "Chiaroscuro: Italians in Toronto, 1815–1915." *Polyphony,* 6, 44–49. Multicultural History Society of Ontario, 1984.

Iacovetta, Franca. *Such Hardworking People: Italian Immigrants in Post-War Toronto.* Montreal: McGill-Queen's University Press, 1992.

Jansen, Clifford. *Fact Book on Italians in Canada.* Toronto: York University, 1987.

Lacroix, Laurier. "Italian Art and Artists in Nineteenth-Century Quebec." In *Arrangiarsi: The Italian Immigration Experience in Canada.* Montreal: Guernica, 1992.

Linteau, Paul-Andre. "The Italians of Quebec: Key Participants in Contemporary Linguistic and Political Debates." In *Arrangiarsi.* Montreal: Guernica, 1992.

Maglio, Antonio. "Salvatore, Filippo." *Tandem News/Corriere Canadese,* December 8, 2002.

Maglio, Antonio. "Over 300 Years of Italians in Canada." *Corriere Canadese/Tandem,* 2002.

Makolkin, Anna. "White Widows, Working Madonnas: The Role of Italian Women in Forging Canada." University of Toronto: Lecture notes, January 31, 2007.

Malam, John. *John Cabot.* London: Evans Brothers Limited, 1997.

Maviglia, Joseph. *A God Hangs Upside Down.* Toronto: Guernica, 1994.

Mazzei, Philip. "Virginia Wine History." http://www.virginiawinewine.org

McLean, Maria Coletta. *Mamma Mia! Good Italian Girls Talk Back.* Toronto: ECW Press, 2004.

"Michelangelo: The Life of Guido Nincheri." http://www.echeat.com/essay.php?t=28255

Micone, Marco. *Immigrant Culture: The Identity of the Voiceless People.* Montreal: Guernica, 1988.

Minni, Dino, and Anna Foschi Ciampolini. *Writers in Transition.* Montreal: Guernica, 1990.

National Congress of Italian Canadians. http://www.canadese.org/

Paina, Corrado. *Made in Canada: The Italian Way.* Toronto: Italian Chamber of Commerce Publication, 2004.

Palmer, Howard. *Immigration and the Rise of Multiculturalism.* Toronto: Copp Clark Publishing, 1975.

Patriarca, Gianna. *Ciao Baby.* Toronto: Guernica, 1999.

Perin, Roberto, and Franco Sturino. *Arrangiarsi: The Italian Immigration Experience in Canada.* Montreal: Guernica, 1992.

Pivato, Joseph. "A History of Italian-Canadian Writing." http://www.athabascau.ca/c11/research/hisitcan.htm

Potestio, John. *The Italian Immigrant Experience.* Thunder Bay, ON: The Canadian-Italian Historical Association/Lehto Printers, 1988.

"Presenza: A New Look at Italian-Canadian Heritage" http://www.civilization.ca/cultur/presenza/pszai01e.html

"Quotes by Prime Ministers: Pierre Trudeau." Canadawiki Can-Quotes. Northern Blue Publishing http://canadawiki.org/index.php/Quotes_by_Prime_Ministers_-_Pierre_Trudeau

Ramirez, Bruno. *The Italians in Canada.* Saint John, NB: Keystone Printing and Lithographing Ltd., 1989.

Ramirez, Bruno. "Workers Without a Cause: Italian Immigrant Labour in Montreal, 1880–1930." In *Arrangiarsi.* Montreal: Guernica, 1992.

Reed, Carole Ann. "Maria Dizio: Setting a Pattern for Success." http://www.mothertongue.ca/community.php?id=1094006096

Ricci, Nino. "A Canadian Love Affair: A Century of a 'Paper for the People.'" *The Toronto Star,* June 4, 1992.

Rochon, Lisa. "A Rare Kind of Developer." *The Globe and Mail,* December 2006.

Salvatore, Filippo. *Suns of Darkness. (Poem for Giovanni Caboto.)* Montreal: Guernica, 1980.

Scardellato, P. Gabriele. "Beyond the Frozen Wastes: Italian Sojourners and Settlers in British Columbia." In *Arrangiarsi.* Montreal: Guernica, 1992.

Scardellato, P. Gabriele. "More than a Century of Toronto Italia." In *College Street, Little Italy.* Toronto: Mansfield Press, 2006.

"A Scattering of Seeds. A History of Italian Immigration to Canada." whitepinepictures.com/seeds/iii/34/history2.html

Serio, Nicoletta. "Canada as a Target of Trade." In *Arrangiarsi.* Montreal: Guernica, 1992.

Shtychno, Alexandra. "Luigi Giovanni Vitale Capello a.k.a. Capello (1843–1902), Itinerant Piedmontese Artist of Late Nineteenth-Century Quebec." Concordia University, 1991.

Stellin, Monica. *The Virtual Piazza.* Toronto: The Frank Iacobucci Centre for Italian Canadian Studies, 2006.

Sturino, Franco. *Contours of Postwar Italian Immigration in Toronto.* Multicultural History Society of Ontario, 1984.

Valle, Gina. "Stereotypes Sell—But We're Not for Sale" and "Legacies." http://www.ginavalle.com

Verdicchio, Pasquale. *Moving Landscape.* Montreal: Guernica, 1985.

Verdicchio, Pasquale. "Italian Canadian Cultural Politics." *Altreitalie.* January–June, #17, 1998.

White, Murray. "The Changing Face of Little Italy." *The Toronto Star,* July 2007.

JOSIE DI SCIASCIO-ANDREWS

Josie Di Sciascio-Andrews was born in Casoli, Chieti in the Abruzzo region of Italy. As a child, she loved reading fairy tales and comic books before graduating to novels. Her family moved to Canada and settled in Oakville, Ontario, where Josie completed high school. She went on to study Italian and French at the University of Toronto and has taught both languages at the elementary and secondary school levels for 26 years. Currently, she is pursuing a masters degree in Italian literature at the U of T. Her poetry and articles have been published in several magazines and anthologies.

DRAGON HILL

Another title from Dragon Hill Publishing...

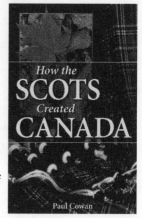